MY
STRONG
TOWER

By Elisabeth Newman

Registered with the IP Rights Office Copyright
Registration Service
Ref: 5343616500

PART 1

The Family

Chapter 1

My purpose in writing this story is to describe how God has brought my family and me through some challenging situations. Without God on our side and supporting us there is more than a fair chance that we would have gone under. He has indeed been my Strong Tower.

Two significant events took place on 12th May 1937, the coronation of King George V1 and my birth. The coronation took place in London while my birth took place in Devon where my father was an Estate Agent. My father had worked for the same employer for just over sixty years having joined the company when he left school at the age of thirteen. In those days this was still reckoned as being unusual

The Estate Agents was called Cooksley's, and it was based at Paignton in Devon. Just before Mr. Cooksley, the owner of the business, passed away, my father visited him as he was very sick. He asked Mr. Cooksley if there was anything that he could get for him. He received a Scrooge-like reply; 'just get me lots more money'. How sad that on the point of death all he could think about was something that he wouldn't have any use for where he was going. My father felt depressed by the answer that he received. On the death of the owner, my dad bought the business from the executors of Mr. Cooksley's estate.

My mother was a stay-at-home Mum as most women were in those days. She was twelve years younger than my father who was thirty-five when they were married. She was quite a good artist, and I loved looking at her beautiful drawings of the ladies fashions that were worn in the 1920's. These had all been done before she married. She was also a brilliant cook and was able to make her own Devonshire clotted cream when we had extra Jersey milk available. My memories of her are that she always had a smiling, happy face. A neighbour called one day and explained that she was worried because she hadn't heard her laughing recently.

We lived in a semi-detached house in Paignton, which is a beautiful part of South Devon with my parents and three younger brothers. George was two years younger than I was and we used to fight a lot. After he had been at school a few years, my parents were struggling with him as he didn't seem to know how to read, write or spell. My parents spent hours trying to teach him and also had a tutor – nothing appeared to help him, but he proved to be very proficient at carpentry. In those days dyslexia wasn't acknowledged. Four years after George, David arrived. He was always full of fun. Two years after him, Dudley arrived. I was eight years old by that time, and I mothered him a lot. Being the eldest, I always got the blame if any of them did something wrong. Apparently, my parents had assumed that I would take care of them and make sure that they didn't do something stupid or break one of our many family rules. I didn't know at the time that is the role of the eldest child in most families. On one occasion I had taken them down to our local beach to get them all out of the house. Dudley went off on his own and was lost. Of course, I was blamed, and, rather unfairly, was in a lot of trouble. Fortunately, he was soon found.

We kept chickens in the garden of our home, and my father used to clip their wings to stop them flying away. I remember on one occasion one tried to fly over the fence into next door's garden. Somehow my father managed to catch it and reduced its wing span even more. I still remember watching, my very cross father, chasing this unfortunate chicken around the garden.

I was two when the Second World War broke out. I do remember a few of the bombings but in our part of the County we escaped most of the raids. There were a couple of instances when the siren went off when I was shopping with my mother and brother in the local town. We ran as fast as we could to our home for cover under the dining room table, my brother loved being pushed in his push-chair at high speed.

One day we were on the way to Brixham, about five miles away, when we stopped at a scenic spot called Windy Corner. We decided to go for a walk along the coast. We had a great view over the bay to Torquay. Suddenly we saw several bombs being dropped. The noise was horrendous and put pressure on our ears. Panic started to grab us. 'Dad what on earth is happening over there?' I asked my father.

My father didn't give me the answer that I expected.

'The German bombers are trying to smash a lot of the houses in the town to pieces. He held my hand tight. 'The planes won't come over here, so we are safe as long as we don't go into the town.'

His voice was calm, which made me feel very safe; however, I couldn't help wondering what would happen to the people in those houses.

On another occasion, we could see the sky was red over Plymouth and Plymouth was a distant thirty miles away. The red sky was from the destruction caused by another bombing raid. We weren't affected much by the war, but it wasn't far away.

There were a lot of evacuee children arriving in our area from London and other cities. We were lucky enough to have a little Jewish girl called Sarah with us for a short time. She had beautiful dark curly hair. It was fun for me to have a girl around to play with. Other children were sent elsewhere in the country. It was during this time that I was caught by our neighbour going in and out of the house through the upstairs casement windows. She reported what I was doing to my parents, and I received a severe ticking off. I had to behave for a while!

Food was rationed during the war and for a few years after hostilities ceased. We had to be careful and use everything wisely with no waste. On many occasions, I offered to help my mother with her baking, but she was convinced that I would waste her precious ingredients. I was banned from baking much to my disgust.

We had a car, but petrol was in very short supply and rationed. We weren't able to go out on many family trips as my father had to use his allocation for his work.

Everything changed when I was nine. We moved to a large Victorian house on a very busy road in the centre of Paignton. When I say that the house was large, I mean that all the rooms were really big. The lounge was situated at the rear of the property, and there was a conservatory attached which stretched into the garden. There was a large dining room in the front with bay windows, a breakfast room, and an adequate kitchen. There were six bedrooms dotted all over the upstairs of the house. The one allocated to me was at the far end of the second floor and was very isolated.

Not long before we moved into our new home, what to me seemed like a palace, our former house had been burgled. My mother had forgotten to lock the back door when she went to pick us up from school one day, and someone had entered the house and taken all the money that could be found. As a result of this incident, I had developed a fear of burglars. When going upstairs at our new property, I would whistle to let any possible thief know that I was on the way, and they should vanish. I don't know what I would have done if a burglar had suddenly appeared. I do however know that my parents would have been too far away to hear me scream, One evening my mother heard me whistling and asked: 'Why are you whistling so loudly in the house?' I felt that she would think I had gone mad if I told her the real reason, so I didn't give her an answer.

'I don't like girls whistling in my home, it's not ladylike,' she added.

I then had to come up with another method of letting burglars know I was on my way to my bedroom. I tried coughing, singing and banging the wall in the hope that the burglars would be put off by that.

It was through this fear that one evening when I was about twelve, I was convinced that there was someone hiding behind the dressing table. I heard some very strange noises. I was so scared that I was going to be killed that I asked Jesus to be my Saviour. I had entered God's Kingdom from being terrified Going to church with my family I had heard lots of sermons on what we needed to do to get to heaven. I had also heard that the alternative to God's Kingdom was hell. Obviously, I was on my own in my bedroom, but it still meant that this was the beginning of my simple childlike faith in Jesus. My fear of burglars was reduced from that point in time.

We had a perfect place to play right on our doorstep as there was a park at the back of the house. We used to spend a lot of time in the public play area there. My mother would go out onto the balcony at the back of the house overlooking the park and ring a cowbell to let us know it was time to come home. Also, she was able to keep an eye on us from the house. Not a good idea from my point of view as she was able to see me climbing tall trees and ignoring her explicit instructions not to do so. I could hear her shouting 'I told you not to climb those trees.' I soon discovered that one of my parent's key intentions was to stop me doing anything that was fun!

When I was about fourteen, I was walking through this park on my own and became aware that someone was following me. I found a bench seat and sat down hoping whoever it was would walk on. Horror! He didn't, he came and sat down next to me. I got up and ran and ran as fast as I could until I arrived home. I still get a shiver down my spine when I hear footsteps behind me.

Chapter 2

Although I don't remember much of my childhood, I do remember that we spent a lot of time on the beach in the summer. During the month of August, we hired a beach hut at Goodrington which was about one mile away from home. The advantage of this was that we didn't have to carry swimming gear, buckets, and spades, etc. every time we went to the beach. We also kept games in the hut in case it started raining, or it got too cold. We could sit inside and play games. It was a lovely sandy beach and safe for swimming in the sea. There was also a boating lake and other attractions. My father would join us for his lunch break having picked up my mother who also brought a picnic. Sometimes some of our friends would join us which made it even better fun. We didn't need to go anywhere else on holidays as we had all we needed at the coast.

Often on a Saturday my Dad would say 'Anyone for Dartmoor?' We would all shout 'Yes' and assist in preparing the picnic. He loved long walks on the moors, and I particularly liked climbing Hay Tor and other rock outcrops. I also liked going on the stepping stones that went across the River Dart. The challenge was to get across without getting my feet wet. Another challenge was to see if I could push my brothers into the water. The water was beautifully clear and the sound of the water going over the stones was very soothing. Another fact I still remember to this day were the beautiful ponies on the moor.

My mother would call out 'Don't stand behind those ponies as they might kick you.' I didn't need any further encouragement to stand well clear as I certainly didn't fancy being kicked by the hind legs of a pony. Also if you got too close, the smell was yuck!

As we had this vast house, we often had visitors come to stay. My brothers and I used to love to play simple tricks on them. Our favourite was to make an apple-pie bed. We made this by folding the top sheet on the bed in half so as it was very difficult to get in! Another trick was to put a bag of flour on the top of the door so that when it was not entirely closed whoever opened it wider to walk through would be showered with flour. We were not very nice children.

Occasionally we had a large family come and stay. There were nine children in this family, so there was wall to wall children for the period they were with us. These children were all given set jobs to do by their mother and their parents were very strict and made sure they did them. This use of the children was not good news for me. In the days following their visit my mother would say; 'Elisabeth, you must do some chores around the house, just like the children who had just departed did. 'They are a good example for you.' I didn't approve of this idea at all. Luckily, after a few days, my mother would forget about the idea and things returned to normal

It was sometime after we had moved to this house that my mother was introduced to the advantages of an automatic washing machine. As far as I can remember it was a Bendix. It was incredible watching the clothes swirling around in the soapy water. No rinsing or having to squeeze water out of the items. We were very lucky as most families couldn't afford one of these as they were expensive. It was a great boon to my mother as there was a lot of clothes requiring washing on a weekly basis.   Before the arrival of this new machine, the laundry was done in a wash tub, with the rinsing done in the sink. Finally, everything had to be put through the mangle. It was nearly a full day of backbreaking work for my long-suffering mother.

When I was eight years old, my Grandparents moved to live close to us in Paignton. They had lived in London where Grandpa had worked for a large insurance firm. He had just retired when he moved. We saw them frequently.   My Granny was good fun and would sometimes put a sixpence in my hand and say 'Don't tell Grandpa.' They had a beautiful upright grand piano which I used to love to play. Although we had a piano at home, I much preferred playing on the grand. The sound was brilliant. How I longed to be able to read music and play well, but mostly I played by ear.   One of my hopes as a child was that I would somehow inherit this piano, but, alas, it went elsewhere

Granny suffered from some form of heart disease and had what I was told were heart attacks. Luckily she seemed to recover quickly.   I was surprised when someone referred to her as the 'resurrection sister.' I guess this meant that it looked like she was dying one day and the next day she was alive again.   She lived until she was well into her eighties.

Grandpa was a bit like a Sergeant Major – a no-nonsense sort.   He, unfortunately, passed away very suddenly in his seventies surprising us all as we had expected Gran to die off before him.

The Christian side of my upbringing was in the Plymouth Brethren. My parents were in a section of the Brethren which had been established in the early 1800's by a man named Mr, Darby. He and another man named

Mr. B Newton felt called to leave the established Church and start a new group of non-conformist Christians. Mr. Darby, together with a number of others, which included Mr. Newton, was dissatisfied with the Anglican Church. In particular, they disagreed with having any specific title or hierarchy. In 1829 this group of like-minded Christians started meeting in Plymouth, Devon. As a result, they became known as Plymouth Brethren. This group met and developed their new way of worshipping over a number of years.

Unfortunately, there was a very strong difference of opinion between Mr. Darby and Mr. Newton on some doctrinal matters. After much discussion and disagreement, a major split occurred. The group, who were against any contact with other Christians, became known as the Exclusive (or Closed) Brethren. The other group was known as the Open Brethren. My parents belonged to the Exclusive group which meant that we were encouraged and in fact forbidden to have any contact with other Christians. We also weren't allowed to do certain specified activities or travel to certain places.

An example of this was when I asked, 'Why can't I go dancing?' The reply was;

'Because Brethren don't do that sort of thing, it leads to sin.'

Life was very structured and governed by a multiplicity of rules. Having grown up in an Exclusive Brethren family, I knew nothing else and automatically accepted the restrictions. We couldn't have friends unless they belonged to this group of brethren so at least having three brothers we were able to make our own fun and games. On Sundays, there were three meetings we had to attend. Also, we were not allowed to read anything other than the Bible or Christian books. I was not allowed to knit, and there were restrictions on many other activities. It was of course before most people had a television but we weren't allowed to have a radio or listen to worldly music. We were allowed to have a daily newspaper and my father always bought the Daily Telegraph. I haven't a clue as to why he chose this particular 'paper, I suppose that it was personal choice. A lot of the time I thought that my life was normal, that is, until I chatted with other girls at school and work. I naturally found out that they were allowed to do all sorts of things that I was not permitted to do, such as going to a fair or a circus.

When I was in my teens, I remember a girl asking me if I would go to the cinema with her to watch a Norman Wisdom film. Of course, this was not allowed. I had been told that if I went to a movie, it was possible that Jesus might return at that very moment and find me in a Cinema – and then what! It was when I started senior school and hearing what other girls of my age were allowed to do that big questions came into my head. Why, why, why couldn't I go to the fair or the firework display? The answer was always the same 'Because brethren don't go to those sort of places.'

Although my parents were strict, they were also very loving and caring. As a family unit, we often had great fun. I am so grateful to God for them.

I am told that when I was three years old, I disappeared from a brethren meeting in Brixham. My father was looking after me but got chatting. When he discovered that I wasn't still present at the meeting, he panicked – I was nowhere to be found. Folk searched the building and all around the area. I was eventually found a couple of miles away walking in the middle of a road in front of a car! The driver of the car evidently got out and went to a nearby house where they took me in. I was told later that there were a lot of children in this family, and they were very disappointed when I was taken away and joined up with my parents. No one had a clue how I had got so far away. I must have got fed up with the goings on at Brethren meetings at an early age!

I had attended a private prep school until I was eleven. I was then expected to take the 11 plus exam to see if I would be bright enough to go to the Grammar School. Well, I had decided that I was not going there even if I had the brains to pass. Why? Because, a girl, who was a little older than me and went to the same Brethren meeting, was at the local Grammar School. She was a real 'goody goody'. I could imagine her taking great delight in telling my parents all the naughty things that I got up to at school. Not what I would want to happen!

Of course, I failed this exam, and I was sent to a secondary school for a short time until my Grandfather put his foot down. He said that I was beginning to speak like a commoner. In fact, I was simply speaking with a Devonshire accent. A grandchild of his was not allowed to speak any other way but 'properly.' The compromise was for me to go to a private school in St.Marychurch, Torquay called Hampton Court School. It was a lovely building with large sports grounds and a path to walk along to reach the cliffs above Babbacombe beach. Years later it was renamed Abbey School. I enjoyed sports there, particularly tennis and netball. Unfortunately, I had a resistance to working hard at the academic subjects. The usual remarks in my school reports were 'She talks too much, and, could do better.' Some folk would say that I've always had a problem as a result of talking too much!

Occasionally we managed to create situations where we had some fun. One day I was in a classroom full of pupils under the supervision of the history teacher. We discovered that the door to the classroom had been locked from the outside. We had no way of getting out. Eventually, the door was unlocked, and we could escape. Four girls were blamed for the action and were made to stand on the landing. Unbelievably I was one of the girls accused and stood on the landing for ages until they found out that I couldn't have done it. I was one of the pupils locked inside the room. Can't understand why they would think I would do such a thing!

I left school at sixteen with the intention of becoming a nursery nurse. For some reason, I loved little children. To achieve my objective, I would have had to go to Tunbridge Wells to train. Oh dear, my father would not allow this on religious grounds. He insisted that I went to a local private secretarial college where he could keep an eye on me. The course was very intense and lasted six months. Although it wasn't the course that I wanted, I decided to apply myself and learn all I could. The six months would go quicker that way. Thankfully, the effort I put in was reflected in the excellent marks that I attained. I probably learnt more English on this course than I had during the whole of my school years! I enjoyed the typing and was good at it and able to achieve the targeted speeds. Shorthand was more difficult, but I still managed to attain the right standard in that.

Once the course had finished, I had to establish what job I wanted to do. I didn't want to work within four walls like my cousin who worked in a Solicitors' Office. I personally couldn't think of anything more boring. Guess what? I ended up working in a Solicitors' Office and, to my great surprise, enjoyed it. It wasn't long before I was promoted to the position of Secretary to one of the partners.

This office was next to my father's Estate Agents, and these Solicitors, where I now worked, had a lot of business contact with him. I knew that if I misbehaved (in my parents' eyes), it would get back to him. On one occasion I was persuaded to place a bet on a horse and guess what – it won! I received quite a lot of teasing; 'just wait till your father hears about your win' they joked. Mercifully, I don't think he ever did. Payday was always on a Friday when I had 'real money.' Occasionally I would go with a girl who worked in my office, to shop in Torquay. We would jump on a bus and pop over there in our lunch hour to see what we could buy in the way of new clothes. Torquay had much better shops than Paignton.

My first real holiday was in 1956 when I was nineteen. I was invited to go to Versailles to stay with a mother and daughter who had been evacuated to Brixham during the war and had stayed with my mother's best friend. We used to see a lot of them and took them out and about when we could. We had kept in touch by letters after they returned to France after the war. The daughter, Claudine, was a few years older than me and spoke perfect English. I had never flown before, so this was a new experience. I caught a plane from the tiny Exeter Airport. It was just a small plane in those days and a great adventure on my own. It was all very exciting. Claudine took me to all the famous places in Paris as well as the palace at Versailles. As a result of her excellent English, I didn't have to use the little French I had learnt at school. It was a great experience and a fabulous holiday.

Chapter 3

As part of my membership of the Exclusive Plymouth Brethren, we would sometimes have to go to Fellowship Meetings on a Saturday. We often would meet brethren groups from other areas. It was at one of these Saturday meetings that I met Arthur. We got chatting and enjoyed each other's company. I was twenty at the time and was introduced to him by his sister who was a friend of mine. I particularly liked his tight curly hair. He had recently completed his National Service and was working in a pharmaceutical supplier. He was slightly older than me. He eventually got around to asking me out, and we made an arrangement to go to Cockington for a walk. It is a pretty village in Torquay which is known for its forge and beautiful thatched cottages. A very romantic place to go for our first date! Our quiet walk was ruined when we bumped into two elderly ladies who attended our brethren meeting in Paignton! Oh dear; they soon had us married off and spread the word amongst the Brethren! Despite this bad beginning, our relationship flourished. Arthur managed to get a job in Paignton, so we were able to spend every spare moment together. We had a lot in common. We had both grown up in the Exclusive Brethren.

After going out together for some months, he asked me to marry him. I had no hesitation in saying 'Yes' and we were married in April 1959.

When I woke up on my wedding day I was relieved to see it was a beautifully sunny morning. For some reason, the Exclusive Brethren didn't allow wedding ceremonies in their halls. I believe that this was because they were not licensed to issue the marriage certificate.

The wedding party had to go to Totnes, a Solicitors' Office which was also a Registry Office for the formality of wedding vows, and to make it all legal. I was very nervous as I had never been to a wedding before, and there was no way of practising the ceremony.

I did as I was instructed, and also repeated strings of words, when instructed. I wasn't able to take in much of what was going on or being said. When the official part had been completed, we returned to the Meeting Hall in Paignton for a Service. The hall was packed as we knew quite a lot of the Brethren people around Devon. All I can remember is that I was instructed, by one of the members, to make sure as a dutiful wife that I worked with my hands! Not quite sure what was meant by that but I guess my place was expected to be in the home doing the cleaning and cooking – what fun!

After the service we went to Deller's Restaurant in Paignton and had a lovely reception – my parents had gone to town and had arranged the very best for us. The Brethren wouldn't allow white weddings. It was considered worldly, so I wore a lovely turquoise dress and hat which had been made for me. We also didn't have bridesmaids, but Arthur had a best man.

After our wedding, we had hoped to go and live in Honiton, East Devon. Arthur had been told he had a job there which included a flat. Six weeks before our marriage the job fell through so we had nowhere to live. Arthur applied for jobs all over the country. Miraculously, he had an excellent position offered to him, a long distance away from Devon, in Maidstone, Kent. Our wedding was fast approaching, so we were extremely relieved.

We had a few days honeymoon in Cornwall and then it was back to Paignton to load up my father's car with our wedding presents. There was only just enough room for Arthur and me in the car. As well as the presents there were many other belongings that we had to take to our new home. Even the roof rack was stacked high with boxes.

We ended up living in Maidstone for fifty-five years during which time we had our four wonderful children. First to arrive was our daughter Hilary and our three sons followed, Mark, Paul, and Roger. Fifty-two of these years we lived in the same house. It was a very happy home and was full of memories.

When we initially arrived in Maidstone, we joined the local Exclusive Brethren. They were a very friendly bunch of people, kind and hospitable to us. We soon were attending most of their meetings.

It was later in the same year (1959) that things started to go very badly wrong in the Brethren. Jim Taylor, who was based in America, became the Exclusive Brethren's' leader. On becoming leader, he issued a great number of new rules and regulations. From my husband's and my point of view, many of these new rules were totally unbiblical.

If we hadn't personally heard these new rules being announced by the leaders at our meetings, we wouldn't have believed that Christian believers could be asked to follow such a crazy list of rules. If you dared to question the sanity of the new rules, you would be 'shut up' or 'withdrawn from.' Sadly many families were divided as a result of these new rules with even husbands and wives preferring to separate from each other rather than change their stance. One member of a family might agree to what was being taught, and the others would entirely disagree. For eleven years Arthur and I went along with it, although we were very unhappy with what was going on. My parents, brothers, and grandmother seemed to think it was all fine. I didn't want to be cut off from them so we endured a crazy situation until we couldn't stand it any longer.

We had always enjoyed the times together when my parents came to stay with us. They loved spending time with our children. Sadly the last time they did visit us, there was so much tension in the house that it was a relief when they left. I didn't think I would ever have to endure an experience like that because I loved them so much. The tension was caused by our totally opposed opinions on what was going on in the Brethren. They knew that we didn't agree with a lot of what we were being told to do. While I concealed my feelings, my parents made their feelings obvious. They also understood what the consequences would be if we left the Brethren. It was so sad that we couldn't enjoy our time together. In the past, we had always had great times as a family.

The longer it went on, the more severe and bizarre the rules and regulations became. For example, if I was seen talking to my next door neighbour I would be kicked out of the Brethren. You could not go to a restaurant for a meal as that meal would have been prepared by 'unclean hands'. Celebrating Christmas and Birthdays was banned.

It was all law and no grace. How opposed to the teachings of Jesus. You weren't allowed to eat with anyone who didn't *'belong.'* My Aunt and Uncle were kicked out when they chose to have a meal with their son who had already left. Our nephew was withdrawn from membership because he chose to own a motorbike. It seemed, at one stage, that a new, even whackier rule, would be created on a weekly basis.

A friend frequently popped in to see me and her first words were always; 'Have you heard the latest?'

'No, what is it this time?' I would reply.

She would then give me the latest rule we were supposed to follow.

The members were not allowed to think for themselves or make their own decisions. We were all subjected to a form of brainwashing and a life of fear governed by rules.

It is hard to explain to folk who were not involved why more people didn't object and resign, especially when the rules got more bizarre. The main reason was that we were taught there were no other Christians, and if we left the Brethren, we would be cast into outer darkness. The reality for me was that if we left, we would be cut off entirely from most of my family and close friends who believed in the edicts. It was possible to lose your mortgage and or employment as many worked for these brethren and received mortgages from them.

Many of the more influential members seemed to have plenty of money. We had been able to obtain an interest-free mortgage from two sisters in the Brethren. Fortunately, they resigned at the same time as we did. This occurrence was a miracle in itself.

Fortunately, I have now forgotten most of what went on, but, at the time, it was appalling and so against what is written in the Scriptures. We were forced to attend all the meetings held on Sundays. The first one was at 6.00am (not easy getting four young children ready for that time). Next one was at 9.00am, followed by 12 noon and then 3.00pm. Also, on weekdays, you had to attend a meeting every evening. If you missed a meeting, an attendance officer would knock on your door or 'phone.

Arthur would often go to the meetings in the evenings on his own, while I stayed at home with the children. At the time I remember being very fearful that he would speak up and question something at one of these meetings. This would, of course, mean that we would be kicked out. We would then be isolated and on our own. I dreaded being cut off completely from my parents, two brothers, and my grandmother. We knew this would be the result if we were 'withdrawn from.' I just couldn't imagine life without them. The thought of this ever happening caused me to feel very depressed.

We stuck with it until 1970 simply because I couldn't bear the thought of losing contact with my parents. It was during some special meetings in the UK that year with Jim Taylor that we heard he had been taken ill. We were also told that he had flown home to New York.

After hearing this, I spoke to my mother on the 'phone and asked her if she knew how he was and why he had vanished so suddenly. She didn't give me a proper answer other than to say, 'Oh is that what you have heard.' She chatted for a few more minutes and then focused on how the children were.

A couple of days later, we heard what had happened. Jim Taylor had evidently been quite drunk. He was known to drink heavily, mainly whisky. In addition to being drunk, he had been caught in bed with a married woman. The day after we obtained this information my mother 'phoned, obviously with the intention of finding out what we had been told. I passed on the information to her, and got the response; 'Oh no, that isn't the truth, and even if it was he is a totally pure man and therefore can do anything he wants.' I couldn't believe I was hearing these words from my mother. She told me to speak to my youngest brother Dudley who was the leader of the exclusive brethren in Paignton as he would be able to help me. She handed him the 'phone, and he tried hard to convince me that I shouldn't leave '*The Truth*'. I stuck to what I believed and refused to waver. Our conversation ended very abruptly

This difference of opinion was the last straw for us as a family.

Arthur and I had decided that we couldn't continue in the Brethren as what was being taught was so contrary to the teachings of Jesus in the Bible. I knew what the consequences were going to be, the greatest of these being the loss of contact with my parents and other family members as well as some friends. The Exclusive Brethren had become a cult and were obeying man rather than God.

The leader of the Maidstone Exclusive Brethren arranged a meeting at which he confirmed that the information we had received about Jim Taylor was correct.

It was now time to decide whether we wanted to follow Jesus Christ or Jim Taylor and the Exclusive Brethren. Most people who attended that meeting made the decision to leave. We were obviously one of the members voting to end our membership. By the end of that week, there had been a worldwide split.

A group of us in Maidstone left at the same time. We used to meet in various homes. There were one or two more splits, and finally, a small group of three families decided to attend the local Evangelical Church. This group had been known as the Open Brethren in the past. We were concerned for our children as there had never been any Sunday Schools. It was at this Church that what was involved in being a real Christian was revealed to me.

It took many years to let go of the things we had been taught. I remember someone saying 'Always read what the Bible says and don't just believe what someone tells you. Also, make sure that you know the context'. I found that really helpful and sought to follow it through. I had such a lot of new things to learn and even more things to be unlearnt.

It was hard to grieve the loss of my parents as they were still alive but refused to have anything to do with me or the family. In fact, I kept a joint of pork in my freezer for the day when they might come. Pork was my father's favourite meat! Sadly that day never came.

I didn't know what to do with my feelings at the time. I felt I had to be strong for the family so didn't discuss what was going on inside me.

There were times when some of our friends would be discussing what had happened in the past and mentioning others who we had known who had remained in the Exclusive Brethren. I couldn't enter into these conversations as it was too painful. I wanted to run out of the room and not hear what they were saying.

When it was my birthday, I wondered whether my parents would be thinking about me. I didn't want anything from them. The thought of them deliberately avoiding contacting me made me feel sad and partly spoil what was a happy day.

It was over twenty years before I could talk about it. Whenever someone tried to speak to me about the loss and all that had happened, I would quickly change the subject. The emotional pain of being reminded of the past and the loss was almost unbearable.

Eventually, a close friend of mine came alongside and helped me to express my feelings and talk things through. I felt such a relief as the turmoil had been lifted from me. She pointed out that it was important that I forgave both my parents and brothers as well as Jim Taylor, the creator of all the trouble. I didn't find it easy and spent some time considering the whole issue of what they had done and the pain of the loss they had caused. I wasn't aware that I had any bitterness, but there was real sadness and emotional pain. There were also times when I felt very angry. I remember driving out in the country one day and finding a quiet spot where I poured all my feelings out to God. I asked Him to take them and in exchange to give me His peace and healing. Finally, I laid it all before the Lord who by His grace enabled me to forgive them. This action brought such healing. I often remind myself of how my Lord has forgiven me and this cost Him so much more.

I often thought it would have been easier to cope with the loss if they had all just died. It was devastating and sad to think that the devil had blinded their eyes so that they chose to obey man rather than God. I missed them like mad. They had been selfless and generous parents. I found it too emotional even to look at their photograph until twenty-three years after that time. I eventually managed to place a photo of my parents in a frame with the rest of the family. Because they were still alive, it was impossible to have any sort of closure. I did, however, find comfort in what the Psalmist says in Psalm 27 verse 10 'Though my father and mother forsake me the LORD will receive me.' What a wonderful promise. I have proved that promise to be true. My Heavenly Father means so much to me knowing that He would never forsake or reject me. I can tell Him anything. Including how I feel, knowing that He listens and cares so much for me

In 1996 I was informed that my father had died – he was 96. I received a letter from my brother Dudley just giving me that piece of information. He ended the letter, 'Yours faithfully.' I even received the letter after the funeral!

In July 2004 I received a letter from my other brother David. He was informing me that our mother was very ill with liver cancer. I was very surprised to get this letter and wondered whether this was to give me the opportunity to visit. My first reaction was - 'no way.' I then decided I should pray about it and felt that at least I could make the suggestion of a visit. I immediately wrote to David asking if this was a possibility. I waited for several days for a reply. I had even decided on which day I could go and had everything packed ready for the journey down to Devon. As I hadn't had a reply I 'phoned. David's wife answered the 'phone and told me that my mother didn't wish to see me. Three weeks later I received a letter to say that she had died aged ninety-two, and the funeral had been held.

You are not allowed to go to their funerals if you have left 'The Truth.' Anyway, I was not informed until after these events had happened. A crafty way of stopping anyone attending.

My eldest brother, who had never belonged to the Exclusive Brethren, contacted me on hearing that our mother had died. He had been informed in the same manner as I had. He had contacted David, and it was agreed that he could visit mother. He lived very close in Devon. George would not have been regarded in the same way as I was as he had never belonged to the brethren and therefore hadn't left 'The Truth'. I was so amazed that he did this as he had not seen her for over forty years. When he got the letter informing him that she had died, he 'phoned me to say that there was no way he would have attended the funeral of either parent even if he had been asked. He had been badly treated and, at one point, was made to have his meals up in his bedroom because he was not a member. When he was in the army in Jamaica, my father had written to him saying that he could never return to live in the family home. If this was Christianity, who would want to be a Christian.

He is still very bitter and against all religions. He told me that if he had attended the funeral, he would have ended up physically attacking his brothers. He suggested that the headlines in the local paper would have been; 'Son attacks close relatives at parents' funeral.' He was and is still so angry. How sad and what a lot they have to answer for.

The last time I met my parents was at Heathrow in April 1970. We went as a family to the Airport to meet them as they were returning from America. It was interesting hearing about their trip to the U.S and all that they had done. My brother David had married an American girl, so they had been staying with her parents. This trip occurred a few months before the split in the August of that year.

Some years later there was an occasion when I was in Brixham, visiting an elderly Aunt. I had the sudden urge to see where my parents were living. I had been informed that they had moved house. A friend was happy to drive me around to see if we could locate their home as I wanted to view it from the outside. We had difficulty finding the address and had to stop and ask someone the way. We finally found it. As my friend was driving us down the road, I was trying to find the number of their house. We got to the end of the road and had just stopped at a junction when I saw my father walking down his drive. We had stopped right beside his house, and he was within touching distance. Well, talk about God's spot on timing! I had not intended calling on them as I was sure they wouldn't be allowed to speak to me. However, seeing him so close, I decided to jump out of the car and acknowledge him. I firstly mentioned who I was and asked how he was. His reply was 'Not too bad for an old man'. I asked if I could see my mother. He went inside to get her. I knew I wouldn't be allowed in the house. She came to the front door saying 'Can't talk to you' and slammed the door in my face. It was awful – she didn't look like my mother. I felt that if she had had a gun, she would have shot me. Although this incident was painful, part of me felt sad for them. They had been brainwashed and had been forced to cut off all contact with their only daughter and four grandchildren.

They did, however, live very close to my brothers David and Dudley so I knew they would be cared for by them.

On another occasion, I had again travelled to Devon to see my Aunt. I was going to help her do some decorating. Before she could buy the paint and wallpaper, she asked me to take her to her Bank to get some money out.

Well, I couldn't believe it – it was the same Bank that I remembered my father used to use years ago. Even more amazing was that having gone into the Bank with my Aunt who should be at the desk but – yes, you've guessed it – my father! I purposely placed myself where he would have to pass. Having finished his business, he set off out of the bank. As he passed me, I said, 'Hello father, it's your daughter Elisabeth.' All I got in response was a stony glare. I moved slightly closer to him and repeated, 'Hello Father, it's Elisabeth.'

Again all I got was a stony glare.

It was hard to bear. My Auntie got very angry and expressed her opinion, which didn't help the situation.

The reason I said who I was is because it was several years since he had seen me and he would not be expecting to see me in Devon.

Also, I had changed my hair style from a bun or French pleat to a short-cut to shoulder length, and it was curly. This had considerably changed my appearance.

Chapter 4

Back in the sixties, we had our four wonderful and precious children. The first to arrive was our beautiful daughter Hilary, and she was followed, at regular intervals, by our three sons, Mark, Paul and finally Roger. It was always our wish to have four children, and I also insisted that they were all born at home I had this innate fear of hospitals. All the births were trouble free until Roger was born. He had the cord around his neck twice. Fortunately, the midwife skilfully managed to sort the problem out. She had to continue attending us for longer than is normal, as he was still bleeding from the navel. With hindsight, we now know the reason for this. Eventually, this healed up, and all was well.

When Roger was three-weeks-old, he had whooping cough. The Doctor told me that this should be impossible as I was breastfeeding him. His older brother Mark had been coughing, but as he had been vaccinated, he didn't whoop so we didn't think too much about it. It was scary having such a tiny baby with whooping cough. He used to go blue all over his face and foam filled his mouth. I took him with me wherever I went, picking him up immediately he started coughing. On two occasions I was convinced he had stopped breathing so I took him to the front door and swung him in my arms backwards and forwards to try and get him breathing again. The Doctor was concerned and arranged to visit us at home with a Consultant from the hospital. Fortunately, they decided he would do better at home with good care than if they took him into hospital. He did eventually recover, but it left him chesty for some time.

Hilary was six-years-old when Roger was born. It was like having a nursery school at home. I loved being a 'stay at home' Mum. We didn't have a car in those days, so I had to walk everywhere or take the children on buses, which they loved. It was hard work taking them into the town to do shopping and particularly going home with a pram tray loaded with shopping. It was a large coach built pram. Fully loaded it had a baby inside, a toddler sitting on the end and two small children pulling backwards up the hill as I was trying to push it forward, plus, of course, all the shopping on the bottom tray! The joys of motherhood!

When Roger was a year old Arthur's father kindly gave us a present of his old Austin A35. He thought we might like to use it for six months as it was too old to sell and had six months' of tax left on it. We appreciated his generosity; it was an incredible gift. It totally changed our lives. I now had the pleasure of cramming four young and very excited children into the back. This was before the days of straps.

Thankfully the six months was extended to eighteen months. The car then had to go through the MOT process. Unfortunately, the garage conducting the MOT discovered that there was a large hole under the driver's seat! We didn't have the money to repair the hole to get it roadworthy, so our beloved Austin A35 went to the scrap heap. We were then very fortunate to be presented with a car by a lovely Christian friend. We have not been without one since.

Unfortunately, our budget didn't allow us to purchase many labour saving devices for use around the home, so the car was a real bonus.

Without a washing machine, it would take me almost the whole morning to do the washing and this on most days of the week. We couldn't afford an automatic washing machine until the children were in their late teens. We had a wash tub but then had to rinse all the washing in the sink. The next step was the spin drying with the water going into a bucket. On one occasion Roger, who was a toddler at the time, pulled the bucket away as water was pouring out. Needless to say, I wasn't too pleased when the kitchen was flooded. A neighbour called round to see what was going on as he had heard a lot of shouting from his garden, which backed onto ours! I assured him that I had stopped short of murdering my son!

My Grandmother used to say, 'hard work never killed anyone.' She might be right, but I can assure her that it was very exhausting work!

Patience was a commodity that was in short supply. The children like to remind me of the time I was so frustrated with them that I picked up a dining room chair and banged it on the floor. They didn't know whether to cry or laugh when it disintegrated into a dozen pieces!

We had a good sized garden for the children to play in, plus a side lane where they would go up and down on their bikes and go carts. They also had the usual swings and climbing frame. I would sometimes create a crazy golf game which we could all play together.

In those days it wasn't the norm to send your children off to playschool, so I had them around me until they went to school. It wasn't a problem as I loved having them at home.

Our daughter Hilary took up nursing when she left school. She trained at St.Thomas' Hospital in London. I still remember how upset I got when I had to leave her in that city on her own. I had always wanted a daughter and now, far too quickly, she wasn't at home anymore. I can remember pushing her in our lovely coach built pram when she was a baby over the bridge of the River Medway in Maidstone. I would look at her and think, I could never love another child to the same extent as I loved her. After she had left, even though there were still the three boys at home, it was quiet without her. Breakfast time she always used to tell us of her dreams. We missed her ramblings and fun. She did well, got married young and continued nursing until she started her family of five children – four boys and finally a daughter. She is now a grandmother of three, with another grandchild on the way. I am really proud of who she is, and it is lovely that we see a lot of her now, as she lives only half an hour's drive away since we moved to be nearer to the family.

Our eldest son, Mark, was a keen motorcyclist. I am not too sure how many motorbikes he has owned in his time, but, much to my continued horror, he drove them fast. I could hear him coming from the end of the road! He became a chef, having left school without any idea of what he wanted to do. He was determined to get a job. His first job was in a French Restaurant in Maidstone. He thoroughly enjoyed it there and got a good grounding in his trade. He then moved around the country working in different restaurants to gain experience. Twenty-four years ago he upped sticks and went to Australia. There he met and married a lovely Australian girl. He now has a daughter and son who are both in their teens. Arthur and I have enjoyed going to visit them occasionally. Mark has done remarkably well. He now has his own Modern Asian Restaurant just outside of Brisbane, and he has won several awards.

I feel very proud when I go to eat at Mark's Restaurant when we visit. The food is fantastic although most of the time I haven't got a clue what I am actually eating. I find it somewhat daunting to have to cook for him when they come over here!

As Mark was crazy about motorbikes, Paul is mad about cars. I couldn't even begin to estimate how many he has had. Initially, his cars were old bangers, but he seemed to get a lot of fun out of them. Over the years he has built several cars from kits. Some were built at home, others he assembled in a workshop in Caterham. He worked there off and on for a number of years. His bedroom used to have so many car parts in it that I was amazed he was able to find his bed! We would have car engines and all sorts of bits and pieces scattered around our home and garage. When he was in his early twenties, he completely stripped an old Ford Cortina and then rebuilt it.

Roger is very musical and has played his guitar in several bands over the years. Of course, he used to practise at home. Oh, what a noise. I could never understand how the loudness improved the quality of the music! I jokingly tell him that my deafness is a direct result of him practising so much! He still plays today but not quite so loud!

He has done a variety of jobs and recently qualified as a CBT psychotherapist. This was a great achievement for him and involved having to study really hard.

Chapter 5

Once the family had grown up and didn't need me around so much, I was curious to know what the Lord wanted me to do. My husband had been a prison visitor for some years, and a prisoner, he was visiting at the time, asked him if he could bring his wife in to meet him.

My first reaction was, 'No way; I am not going to that place.' However, unknown to me, God had another plan. Shortly after this conversation, I watched the BBC programme, Songs of Praise, being broadcast from Maidstone prison. Conversations with some of the prisoners made me realise that these men weren't monsters as I had imaged, they were normal men, and God loved them. I began feeling that God did want me to go in and visit.

The following day I was visiting a friend whose husband happened to be a prison officer. He had just called in for his lunch. I told him what I felt and did he think there was anything I could do. His reply was 'Oh yes, we always need people who are willing to visit the prisoners.'

At the end of that week, this officer called on me and said, 'I've just been chatting to one of our inmates who would like to see you. He will be released in about six months' time and can't relate to women.' Oh no, what had I suggested – I suddenly felt quite scared.

That night I prayed earnestly about it and was strongly reminded by God of the verse in Joshua that says: 'Have I not commanded you? Be strong and courageous, do not be afraid; do not be discouraged, for the LORD your God will be with you wherever you go'. That was all the confirmation I needed. I said to the Lord 'OK, if you come into the prison with me, I will go.' So I went through the vetting process to be approved as a visitor. This process involved an interview and filling out the necessary application forms.

Thankfully, I was approved.

My first prisoner was being held in the sex offender's wing. This category of prisoner is locked up in a separate section of the prison for their own safety. He knew quite a lot about Christianity and had listened to Christian programmes on the radio. This was helpful, as we had something in common to discuss. Our relationship didn't appear to be hampered by me being a female. When he was finally released from prison, I went to meet him. Much to my amazement, he threw his arms up in the air and shouted 'Hallelujah I'm free.' He came to church with us on one occasion, but he then moved away. For years afterwards, I received a Christmas card from him. It appeared, from his comments, that he was still doing well and worshipping the Lord.

The second prisoner I was asked to see was very different. The Chaplain thought it would be advantageous if I could visit quite a troubled man. He had recently started going to the Prison Chapel but still had a lot of problems. I prayed about it and finally agreed to meet with him. My first visit was to take place in the hospital wing as this inmate was mentally ill at the time. I was escorted into a side room and was then told that it wouldn't be possible to see him as he was not stable enough to receive a visitor.

The Prison Doctor came in to speak to me and said that this prisoner was walking up and down in his cell saying

'I'm a shepherd, I'm a shepherd'. The Doctor didn't think the prisoner would benefit from talking to me. I suggested that perhaps I could be introduced to him for say, five minutes. The Doctor agreed, and Archie (not his real name) was brought into the side room carrying a bible. After we had introduced ourselves and he told me he had a wife and three daughters, I commented on the fact that he was carrying a Bible. His response was 'Yes and isn't the story of Abraham incredible; he was willing to kill his own son.' Archie couldn't get over how anyone could do that. We chatted about this for a few minutes.

I then told him that God the Father had allowed his Son to be crucified in my place for all the wrong things I had done. His expression seemed to show that he was taking all this in. I continued for a little while telling him the wonderful gospel message. A prison officer was in the room so he too got the gospel message whether he wanted it or not! The five minutes that I had been allowed turned into an hour and a half. This amount of time is the maximum allowed for a visit. Archie was much calmer when I left him.

The following week I saw him again. While I was being escorted to the hospital wing, the officer mentioned that he had noticed Archie seemed quite a bit better. On this occasion, a prison officer sat just outside the door. He would still have heard all that I spoke about. I was telling Archie all about Jesus; who He is and what He has done for us. Archie was hungry to know more.

On the third visit, I was instructed to meet him in the main visitors' hall as there were no officers available to be with us in a separate room. They also told me that Archie seemed considerably better. Soon after we had sat down at a table with a cup of tea, Archie said; 'It may sound a silly question but how do you become born again.'

Out came my little Gideon Bible from my bag and we discussed John chapter three verse sixteen etc. Because of Archie's childhood, I wondered whether he would understand what it meant regarding God loving him so I said to him 'God is absolutely crazy about you'.

His eyes lit up, and he seemed to have an understanding of what I was trying to convey to him. God had created an amazing opportunity to share the gospel. I felt certain that he was the prisoner God wanted me to see. I visited him on a weekly basis for two or three years. I remember going to the Prison Carol Service. He was dressed up in the choir's outfit and looked so pleased with himself.

When he was finally released, he went back to his home in Dorset and continued sending me Christmas cards enclosing letters giving me details of how he had been visiting different churches giving his testimony. What a wonderful God we serve.

After Archie had been released, I continued visiting a couple of short term prisoners. It always amazed me that they insisted on telling me why they were in prison. I had to learn to appear un-shockable at some of the things I heard. After these two inmates had been moved elsewhere, I felt it was right that, after five years, I should discontinue my prison visiting.

I will never forget the next time I led someone to the Lord. The opportunity arose following a meeting I attended at which a lady was talking about 'Home Evangelism'. She told us that she would go knocking on doors telling people the Good News about Jesus. As part of her talk, she shared a few instances of how she introduced some folk into God's Kingdom. At the end of this meeting, I had a great desire to do the same. Jesus meant so much to me so why not share the news with others. I prayed at the end of that meeting asking God to use me to bring someone to know Him. Immediately after praying, massive doubts entered my mind. The devil was trying to make me change my mind. Thoughts like; 'I couldn't possibly do this, I wouldn't know where to start and anyway, who did I think I was to be able to be used in this way.'

About six months after that Meeting I was involved in helping in the establishment of a new children's' club called Saturday Special. It had been agreed that this new club would be run at our church. My neighbours had four children, so it made sense to invite them. We didn't know them very well other than occasionally chatting over the garden fence. I was delighted when they agreed. We had a great start with a lot of children attending. The programme was made up of the usual sort of things; games, puzzles, craft, Bible stories and lots of fun.

On the Tuesday, following that first Saturday, I was just pulling up in the car outside my house when I spotted Val, my next door neighbour, on the path. She was waiting for me when I got out of the car.

Val thanked me for taking the children to the club saying they enjoyed the time. She then said 'What do you believe in your church as I don't believe that Jesus is God or that there is life after death.' (She had been studying with the Jehovah Witnesses for some time).

I didn't answer her then and there but invited her to come and have a chat over a cup of tea. It was evident she was searching for something and came armed with lots of questions. I now believe the Holy Spirit was working in her, but she hadn't found peace with the Jehovah Witnesses. Val would come in every week and was hungry to discuss Christianity more and more. I experienced the power of the Holy Spirit as I shared with her. After about six weeks she finally came to the point of accepting Jesus as her Saviour and prayed asking His forgiveness and for Jesus to come into her life. I was so excited about this I wanted to shout it from the rooftops. As soon as she left that afternoon, I phoned a friend from church who had been praying for Val. I told her the wonderful news. As we were about to finish our conversation I said I had better get on and prepare the dinner. She suggested I made 'Hallelujah pie!' It was and is such an honour and privilege to introduce someone to Jesus.

At that moment Val became, not just my neighbour, but a sister in the Lord as well. She became a dear friend.

Chapter 6

One morning in 1986, as I was driving to an early morning planning meeting for a three week Mission, I felt the Lord was prompting me to start a Christian Counselling Service.

I discussed what I had in mind with a number of church leaders. I selected ones who I felt would be sympathetic to such an idea. Following positive feedback from my discussions, a steering group was formed with nine churches represented. There was much to discuss, and we were unsure of where to start.

We decided to call some of the local churches to a meeting at which we could share the vision. Several people expressed an interest in what we were suggesting and offered to get involved. Prayer was a very important part of the meeting as we wanted to make sure we were doing God's will and to give Him the glory for all that was to be done. Training courses in Basic Biblical Counselling were then arranged, with an encouraging number attending.

We needed to find supervisors, telephone listeners and of course those called to do the actual one on one counselling. A decision also had to be arrived at as to how the project was to be funded. We wanted to be able to offer a free service to folk although they would be asked to make a donation if they could afford it. The steering group had many meetings until finally a smaller Management Team was formed. This latter team consisted of a Treasurer, a Secretary, a Doctor, a representative of the Churches and two counsellors.

At the end of 1990, everything was in place, but there were no premises from which to operate the Service. It had been named Crossline Christian Counselling Service. Funds were also at a low level. We decided to go ahead by Faith. We would commence by offering six hours a week to clients and that this service would start on 31st January 1991.

We looked around for rooms but found nothing suitable. One day somebody mentioned that there was a church building near the centre of Maidstone that might be available. I 'phoned the Pastor, who I knew quite well, and he was delighted to offer me use of some of the rooms when they weren't being used for Church meetings We felt really blessed by this offer, even more so when he said that he wouldn't charge us any rent. Our faith was rewarded, and the counselling service commenced on 31st January 1991.

Soon after we started, I received a 'phone call from a friend who had just completed a counselling training course at Waverley Abbey. She was full of enthusiasm for the course and insisted that I attend the next time the course was run. She stated that she would pay the fee for me. Her kind offer was a wonderful gesture as there was no way I could have afforded to pay for the course. Another miraculous provision from God.

We had been operating from the Church in Maidstone for three years when I received a 'phone call from a Christian G.P. asking if we would like to use some spare rooms that were available in her Surgery. What an exciting development. We had been feeling for some time that operating the counselling service from a Church was keeping non-Christians from approaching us. This new location would solve this problem. We thankfully accepted this offer and moved in.

We used these premises for approximately twenty years when the Surgery had to find alternative premises as their lease was ending. The Christian Doctors and the Manager of this surgery were definite that they wanted Crossline to go with them wherever they happened to move to. Their thoughtfullness was a great boost to us. They had to convince those in charge of the NHS locally that they needed rooms to accommodate the counselling service as well as their own medical needs. As part of the exercise, we had to provide a lot of statistics relating to our work for the Surgery to show the PCT group how valuable our service was. Eventually, news came through that a brand new purpose built surgery was to be built, and a suite of rooms would be provided for Crossline. What a Miracle. We were told it was unheard of for the NHS to agree to let a Registered Charity, a Christian one at that, use rooms in an NHS funded building. Even more amazing it was rent free! How good is our God! Packing up in preparation for the move was just like moving house. I had plenty of decluttering to do having run this counselling service for twenty-three years. We finally moved into this new Surgery building in July 2013. There were four rooms specifically assigned to Crossline. By this time we had a team of thirty voluntary counsellors.

We had started in a small way by offering a counselling service for six hours a week. It wasn't long before we had to extend our hours until eventually; we were available all day, every day of the week. These extended hours meant that I was working practically full time.

It has been an incredible privilege to be involved in this work. As coordinator of the service for twenty-three years in addition to counselling and supervising, I finally decided it was time to retire at the age of seventy-six.

I was given the most amazing surprise leaving party. The team of Counsellors and my successor had put in a tremendous amount of work into preparing my leaving gift. They did a presentation entitled – '*This is Your Life in Crossline – January 1991 to December 2013*'.

They had also put the presentation into a book format which will always be a lovely reminder of all the folk with whom I worked. They had been like a second family, and I knew that I would miss them all terribly.

I am still involved, but only as a Trustee. If I was God, I certainly wouldn't have chosen me to do this work. It has proved to me that He equips those he calls to serve him.

PART 2

Chapter 7

It was great fun, as well as hard work, having four children. They played and fought together like any normal healthy family. One of their favourite games was to see how high on the stairs they could jump from and which one would have the highest score. I did feel sorry for my neighbour as it made quite a noise with interspaced loud bangs as they hit the bottom, but she never complained, in fact, she told me she loved to hear the children.

 After both Paul and Roger had started to walk, I often noticed that they had a fair amount of bruising. It was particularly noticeable as the two older children didn't seem to have more than would be expected when playing rough and tumble games together. It was when either Paul or Roger was limping and appeared to be in pain that I became concerned.

On one occasion, when Paul was obviously in pain and limping, I took him to see the G.P. The Doctor amazed me when she said, "He is probably copying someone he had seen limping or may be doing it to get attention." I was far from happy about this suggestion. It was obvious to me, as their mother, that neither of these ideas was correct.

On another occasion, when Roger was struggling to walk, I took him to our local hospital. The comments on his condition were similar, but on top of these, the Doctor drew my attention to the fact that he had a lot of bruising. Comments were also made regarding the amount of bruising they both had. Fortunately, we were not referred to the Social Services. I can't imagine how devastating that would have been. My mind was beginning to go frantic I kept asking myself "What was wrong with them?"

As their mother, I knew that something was not right.

One day when I was busy in the kitchen, Paul, who was four at the time, was romping around on the landing with his brothers when he banged his mouth on a chest of drawers. He had knocked a tooth loose which started to bleed. There were shouts from the other children "Mummy, come quickly; Paul is bleeding." Upstairs I ran to find blood coming from his mouth. After a while, I 'phoned the Dentist who wanted us to go and see her. She was sure that it would settle down in a couple of days. She asked us to contact her again if there was still a problem after that time. Well, after he was oozing blood for three days I contacted the Dentist again, and she wanted me to take Paul to see her. With this, she decided that it was not going to settle down, and the best thing would be to take the tooth out as it was quite loose, so out it came. It was then that the bleeding became really heavy. After a while, he was becoming very drowsy, and I had to try and stop him from going to sleep. I quickly realised this could be serious and took him to the local hospital when a Doctor immediately referred him to East Grinstead Hospital where they specialise in difficult dentistry. This was about one hours drive away. We had quickly to make arrangements with friends to look after the other three children during the daytime. It was horrible having to leave Paul in hospital, but we had to get back in time to give the others tea and put them to bed. When we got back home, we found that a kind neighbour had come into the house and had washed all the bedding which had been soaked with blood. I was so grateful as I would probably have binned the lot. It had been a horrible mess. Eventually, the bleeding stopped, but Paul was still very weak as he had lost a lot of blood.

After a couple of days, they transferred him back to Maidstone Hospital which made life easier for all of us. It was a huge relief when Paul was finally strong enough to be allowed home to be with the rest of the family particularly as Hilary and Mark had gone down with mumps, and I needed to look after them.

I was hanging out the washing one morning when Roger came looking for me. He was limping badly and crying saying 'Mummy my foot hurts.' He was two at the time. On examining his ankle, I noticed that it was very swollen and warm. Off we went to the hospital.

The Doctor on duty was not only concerned about the pain but also that he had a high temperature. Again there were comments about the amount of bruises he had which increased my anxiety. As he was running a high temperature, they decided to keep him in under observation and to ensure that he didn't try to walk and put pressure on this joint. He was there for three days. He screamed and screamed when I left him each day – it was so hard to leave him so young in the care of someone other than me, his mother. Unfortunately, I had no option. The nurses assured me the following morning that he had settled down soon after I left.

It was during this time that they took some blood tests from both Paul and Roger. I wasn't very medically minded and managed to convince myself that it must be leukaemia. I remembered that I had read somewhere that one of the symptoms of leukaemia was bruising.

The thought of this being a possibility freaked me out. This sort of thing happened to other people, not us. We were a healthy family. Then a week after the blood test came the 'phone call asking me to make an appointment to see a Doctor and get the results. It was then that they told me that both Paul and Roger had haemophilia.

I began to feel very confused at this information as I had never heard of this condition. The Doctor explained that it was a bleeding disorder where the blood doesn't clot because a protein normally made by the body to help make blood clot is either partly or completely missing. The missing protein is a clotting factor and is known as Factor 8. I was informed that they would require intravenous injections of this clotting factor whenever they had a bleed. Roger's painful and swollen ankle had been a result of the effects of haemophilia.

It was explained to me that most of the bleeding problems are internal – either into muscles or joints which over time causes crippling pain and damage to whichever joint or muscle is affected. If they passed a lot of blood, this would be classed as an emergency, as would a bang on the head. In any of these cases, they would need urgent treatment.

They were both diagnosed as very severe by their level of clotting factor. This was 0.01 for both Paul and Roger. The level for someone without haemophilia is between 50 and 150. Haemophiliacs are male while the disorder is passed down by the female carrier.

There is no trace of haemophilia back in my family so I had no idea that I was a carrier of this disorder. Evidently, approximately 30% of cases start without any history. The daughter of a haemophiliac will be a carrier which means that if she gives birth to a son, he may have haemophilia. A sister of a haemophiliac has a 50/50 chance of being a carrier. A carrier will need Factor 8 cover if having an operation, teeth out or accident otherwise small bleeds tend to clot after a time without any treatment. They normally have a lower than normal clotting factor but not as low as a haemophiliac.

When I was nine years old, I had my tonsils out and evidently woke up in a pool of blood. Many years later I realised why. I occasionally had problems with my ankles after playing tennis, netball or other sports. I also had frequent heavy nose bleeds and real trouble when teeth were taken out – the gums had to be stitched to help control the bleeding. Other than that I don't remember being ill except the usual childhood illnesses. I don't remember my parents or brothers having any medical problems.

I started researching this blood disorder and was interested to discover that Queen Victoria had been a carrier. Her eighth son, Prince Leopold had haemophilia. He died aged thirty. Two of her daughters were definitely carriers and possibly another one. As they all had large families haemophilia was passed down to several European royal families. The most well known are Alexis, son of Nicholas II Tsar of Russia and his wife Alexandra who was the granddaughter of Queen Victoria.

Bleeds into joints and muscles cause tremendous pain which in time can result in disabilities particularly if not treated promptly. Roger once explained it well by saying, when he had an ankle bleed, that it felt like someone had got hold of his foot and was pulling it as hard as possible.

I have heard it said that most toddlers fall down the stairs at least once. They seem to be able to bounce back and after an initial yell soon recover. Not so with Roger.

When he was about two and a half, not long after he had been diagnosed with haemophilia, he fell down the stairs. It was a day or so after that he passed a large amount of blood. Down to the hospital again we went, and they agreed to keep him overnight under observation. When visiting him the next morning, I was told he was fine as he had had a good night's sleep. It sounded to me as if they thought I was a neurotic mother making a fuss. A few minutes later just as the Doctor was walking along the ward to see another child, Roger said he wanted to go to the toilet. He then passed another lot of blood. They then believed me, and Roger was given treatment. I have often wondered why mothers are not always believed by the so-called 'experts.'

Leaving either of the boys in hospital was really hard, particularly when you could hear screams begging me to stay. When reaching home, I would 'phone through to the Ward to see if the screams had stopped. I was always assured that they had, and they were happy playing with toys.

Chapter 8

Having had the diagnosis we were told to go to the Churchill Hospital in Oxford where we would be registered, and they would keep our records. Having made the journey, I found this time to be really helpful. I was given very clear information as to what to do when certain problems occurred and the approximate amount of Cryoprecipitate units that should be given intravenously depending on each situation.

We were also given a list of hospitals in the UK which had haemophilia centres. This information was essential if we wanted to go away on holiday.

Cryoprecipitate (Cryo for short) was a blood product prepared from plasma and contained clotting proteins. Unfortunately, it was a very crude form of clotting factor which could cause some very unpleasant reactions.

Before the early 1960s, boys rarely grew to be men. The only treatment they would have had then was ice packs and bed rest. It was about the time that Paul was born that Cryo started to be used.

We continued to go to our local hospital for treatment which was not too successful as it appeared that Paul and Roger were not always given enough units of Cryo for clotting and insisted on too much bed rest which would mean that it could cause stiffness and eventually arthritis. It was important to get the balance right of bed rest and gradual use of an affected joint or muscle. When weight-bearing joints are affected, it takes much longer to get back to being able to walk again.

Having been informed by the Haemophilia Specialist at the Churchill Hospital in Oxford as to how many units of Cryo would be needed for certain bleeds, it was very frustrating when, in my opinion, the local hospital were not giving them enough Cryo to control the bleeding. The Paediatric Doctor would never discuss anything with me regarding the boys' situation and treatment. Fortunately, there was a lovely Sister on the ward, and she would come over and chat with me. She was able to fill me in with any information she had. Many years after we had left that hospital I met this Sister in town. I was amazed that having worked with a lot of children in her time, she remembered us. Her first question was 'How are the boys?' She had always been very interested in what was going on. It may have been that they were the first haemophiliacs they had had on the ward – I don't know.

School in the infants and juniors was really tough for Paul and Roger as they were not allowed to go out to play or participate in any rough sports which could so easily cause internal bleeding. I remember on one occasion Roger was really upset about all

this and said: 'Life is not worth living if I can't go out to play with my friends.' What a horrible statement to hear from one's child. It was the advice given to us to protect them against possible bleeds.

I had told their respective teachers in the primary school that they were not to treat them as a special case if they needed to punish them for bad behaviour. I felt it was important that they were treated the same as any other child.

I just hated seeing them have needles stuck into their little veins. It seemed so cruel. When they were older, I agreed that, within reason, they could decide for themselves whether they wanted to do certain activities in the knowledge that they were likely to suffer afterwards.

One Friday morning, while I was doing some baking, I heard Paul screaming. He was five years old at the time. He had climbed onto a chair outside the dining room window, and, yes, he had fallen off onto the concrete path. He had cut the inside of his mouth and, of course, there was a lot of blood. Down to the hospital again and after treatment, it was decided that he should go to the Churchill Hospital in Oxford. An ambulance was organised, while I made arrangements for the rest of the family to go to friends. The ambulance driver was a Christian, although I didn't know this at the time. I have met him at Christian events several times since that day. He has always reminded me of this trip as the nurse on board refused to let him stop to have his lunch! Fortunately, we had some friends who lived in Oxford who were happy for us to stay with them for the weekend. I hated leaving Paul in the hospital again. With the correct amount of Cryo, the bleeding soon stopped and after a while, we were allowed to take him home. Fortunately, my husband had driven up to be with us so that we could all go back together.

We carried on attending our local hospital, mainly because I was too scared to drive to London to a main Centre. It was a thirty-five-mile drive each way. The other advantage of being treated in our local hospital was that Arthur, who worked locally, could visit after work. This arrangement meant that I could return home to be with the other children.

We were fortunate having neighbours who helped out by picking the children up from school when I was unavailable to do this. They were a lovely retired couple who loved our children as if they were their grandchildren.

When Paul was seven, he had had a bleed in one of his ankles. Although having had some treatment at the local hospital he was still unable to walk after three weeks and was in considerable pain. As a result, he was off school again. After this time, I contacted the hospital to ask for crutches as he was heavy to carry around for long. I was told to bring him down to the hospital, which I did. The Doctor got hold of his foot, twisted it around, and said he should have been going to school all this time. To twist his foot was the worst thing she could have done. I was furious and 'phoned the Haemophilia Centre at the Churchill Hospital in Oxford. They instructed me not to go back there but to go to St.Thomas' in London. They made an appointment for that afternoon. I had no time to get scared about driving in London (I had never driven there before). I quickly organised for the other children to be looked after and also found a friend to accompany us; mainly to read the road signs for me. We then set off and, to my amazement, arrived safely. It was obvious the staff knew what they were doing which was such a relief and gave me confidence. Paul had to attend St.Thomas' regularly for many weeks before he could walk again unaided. As a result of not having had the right treatment at our local hospital, lasting damage had been done to his ankle. The joint had become very weak which caused frequent bleeds until he was eleven. He was then able to have an operation to fuse the joint.

My first experience of driving in London had been memorable. Firstly I had to find somewhere to park. Not easy, especially as I had to carry Paul. Eventually, I found what I thought was a space under a railway bridge not too far from the hospital. I checked to see if there were any yellow lines and couldn't see any. When we returned to the car, there was a ticket on it. I was furious. There evidently were yellow lines, but they were so covered by dirt that they were impossible to see. I appealed, and the fine was cancelled. What a relief. Unfortunately, it was rush hour when we left, and the traffic was horrendous. It took us three hours. I was exhausted when I finally got home. Normally it would take about an hour and a quarter. After driving there many many times, I learnt to drive like a Londoner when in London. Following that first visit, I was given a pass to use the Hospital car park. Being able to park in the hospital grounds was such a help, particularly when Paul or Roger was unable to walk except with crutches due to bleeds in their lower limbs.

Soon after we had started going to St.Thomas' we were asked to attend as a family as they wanted to carry out blood tests on us all. When it came to my husband's turn, he had vanished. We looked along the corridors and eventually he turned up looking a bit green. How he hated even seeing the needle! These tests proved that Arthur and Mark were clear of haemophilia but that Hilary and I were carriers. We already knew that Paul and Roger had been diagnosed as positive.

During one of our visits to St.Thomas' the Professor we were under wanted to speak to me. He said, 'In a few years' time there will be a home treatment process introduced.' He explained this meant that I would be able to do all their intravenous injections on my own at home. I promptly replied, 'There is no way I could possibly do that.' I was horrified at the thought of it. How on earth could I inject my own young boys?

The Professor said, 'If drug users can inject themselves so can a normal intelligent human being'.

I was not sure about the 'intelligent' bit, but I was still very wary of ever having to do this. I guess he was just trying to give me confidence.

My trips to London were often two or three times a week with one or other of the boys. This put a great strain on us, both financially and physically. My husband, although employed full time, took on two extra small part-time jobs to help with the expenses. Those were the days before there was any attendance or mobility allowances.

I remember on one occasion we had to go to St.Thomas' twice in one day. We had almost got home after Roger had received a Cryo injection when he started screaming in the back of the car. He said it felt as if his whole body was on fire. Back we went to London.

After several years going backwards and forwards to London, the time finally arrived when I had to learn how to do these intravenous injections. My training was done under the watchful eyes of Doctors or nurses. Wow, it was scary; however, the boys had and, in fact, still have very good veins which helped. The new process was introduced just as I felt I was at the end of my tether. I simply had to stop the trips to London. God knew that all this travelling was getting too much for me and I firmly believe He stepped in just at the right time. What an amazing God; I was so grateful to Him.

The home treatment made such a difference to our daily life. As soon as there was internal bleeding of any kind I was able to inject whoever needed it. It also gave many long term benefits. If there was heavy external bleeding, the injections also helped.

At last, we could make some arrangements to go out for a day or even away. We would always take a pack of Factor 8 with us in a cool bag. Before home treatment, there were many times we had to cancel arrangements due to having to make yet another hospital visit. Cancelling trips at the last moment was tough as we felt that we had to let people down. Being on home treatment also meant that the boys would be able to attend school more often. To date, they had missed so many days.

The reason we were able to carry out the treatment at home was that we were not using Cryo anymore. This product had been replaced by freeze-dried Factor 8 which shouldn't give any side effects. Fortunately, I didn't have a problem seeing blood. I was used to having to deal with heavy nosebleeds and a lot of bleeding when teeth had to come out. Unfortunately, my husband couldn't stand the sight of blood or the needles and would exit the room like a shot.

If nothing else, I had to learn a lot of patience (I am naturally very impatient). Both boys objected to having the injections, and it could take quite a while before they would co-operate. I often resorted to bribery. If they co-operated, they would be rewarded with a Matchbox Car or a Ladybird book. On one occasion in the hospital it had taken four adults to hold Roger down while a Doctor tried to inject his arm. This occurred when he was three or four. One time, after we were on home treatment, Roger again had a nasty joint bleed. Despite being in a lot of pain, he was making it very difficult for me to get the needle into his vein. Every time I was nearly there, he pulled his arm away. I was attempting to inject him for close on three hours! In the end, I told him I would 'phone the hospital, and they would say that he had to stay in. Also, I would have to return home and leave him there. Off I went into the other room to get the 'phone. I picked it up pretended to speak to the hospital in a loud voice. It wasn't long before Roger called out, 'it's all right Mummy you can inject me.' At last, the needle went in OK. What a relief. I was exhausted.

All the time they were at school I was practically housebound as I had to be available in case I was required. Fortunately, this wasn't a big problem for me as I loved being at home. Also, a large family needed a lot of looking after, so I was always busy. I had to be available in case the school secretary 'phoned. I would then go and collect whichever one had the bleed. Off to the hospital we would go or home after we started the home treatment. This had gone on for several years when a dear friend gave me a pager. I could now be contacted if I was out. This was really helpful and gave me a little more freedom. I could then shop without having the children trailing along behind me which would take twice as long. Mobile 'phones had not been invented at this stage. What a difference one of those would have made to my life!

Chapter 9

In 1976, some friends, very generously suggested that we went on holiday with them to Swansea for two weeks. They had rented a large house which would easily accommodate two families. Our friends had three children of similar ages to our children so it was a good match. The first week was a real treat. We all got on well together.

On the Monday of the second week, we joined up with another family known to our friends. This family had four children. It was suggested that we all go to the Brecon Beacons for the day. It was a beautiful sunny day, and the scenery was amazing.

We parked our cars in a car park and started strolling through lovely woodlands. The summer sun shining through the trees made a magnificent picture. What a reminder of our great Creator this was. Occasionally we could hear the sound of a stream running over rocks and then there was a waterfall which we all stopped to watch and listen to for a few minutes. It had been raining during the night, and everything smelt lovely and fresh. The adults enjoyed chatting as we ambled. The children were running and jumping around. They seemed to be having great fun together. Suddenly we heard voices shouting from below the cliff. We couldn't hear what they were saying, but they sounded desperate.

We walked over to the edge of the cliff and could now hear a man shouting, 'a child has fallen over the cliff.'

The child in question was our eight-year-old Roger. He had been trying to catch up with the older children and got too near the edge. He tried to clutch hold of grass on the edge, but it came away in his hand, and he had gone over the cliff. He ended up face down in a stream which contained large stones. He had fallen between thirty and forty feet. The people who had gathered down by the stream had picked Roger up and were carrying him. We clambered down and met them. It was very steep so it was quite tricky. The couple who rescued Roger were accompanied by their two teenage sons. They told them to run as fast as they could to the telephone box which was located back at the main road and 'phone for an ambulance.

If this family hadn't been down by the stream, it doesn't bear thinking about what could have happened. Carrying Roger between us was very painful for him. Every part of his body seemed to hurt. Our daughter, Hilary, who had recently done a First Aid Course noticed that his arm was broken. As we walked back to the road, we met some walkers who kindly offered us their rug as a makeshift stretcher. It was now much easier to carry him.

By the time we arrived at the road, the ambulance had arrived.

I informed the Doctor that my son suffered from haemophilia and needed to go to Cardiff Hospital as they had a Centre for Haemophiliacs. The Doctor said they would take him to the nearest hospital which was Neath as he wasn't bleeding. Little did he know. He obviously had little knowledge of the internal bleeding problems of haemophiliacs.

When we arrived at Neath Hospital, I asked if I could contact the Haemophilia Centre at St.Thomas' Hospital in London to check the amount of Factor 8 my son should be given. The reply was, 'wait until the x-ray has been carried out and he has been thoroughly examined.' Roger was in agony, and other patients could see he was in a lot of pain. Some even offered to let him be seen in front of them. This was not agreed to by the medical team. We were informed that he would have to wait his turn. Finally, they confirmed he had broken his arm, and they would put it in a cast. By the time all this had been done the people at St.Thomas' Haemophilia Centre had gone home at the end of their workday. I would have to work out how many units to give him myself and trust I was giving him the right dosage.

Arthur had to drive back to Swansea to the house where we were staying to get the supplies of Factor 8 that were needed. This took some time as he didn't know the roads around this area. He had requested a police escort, but this was refused. He finally managed to get back to the house where we were staying and then back to the hospital. I was so relieved when he got back. Meanwhile, the friends we were with looked after the other three children.

While I had been waiting for the Factor 8 to arrive, Roger and I had been placed in a large room on our own. Roger was lying down on a couch, and it was obvious something serious was going on as his abdomen was swelling alarmingly.

A Doctor came in every now and again to check his blood pressure which was dropping. As soon as Arthur arrived with the Factor 8, I made it up and then the Doctor tried to get the needle into a vein. He tried several times without success until finally, he agreed that I should do it. Fortunately, the needle went into the vein first time. I don't think the Doctor was too happy that I had been able to do this and he hadn't! After a while, in fact, it was three hours after the x-ray, we were told that we would be taken to another Hospital. Oh no, I thought, I just prayed that it would be Cardiff. On enquiring whether this was the case, I was told he would be going to Morriston Hospital. My heart sank as I thought we would have the same problem of not having the right expertise available.

We were placed in an ambulance with a first-year student nurse; she was to travel with us. She could see Roger was almost unconscious, and she said that she didn't feel comfortable accompanying a child who was in such a bad way. The Doctor decided to come with us after all. We were blue-lighted with the siren going all the way. After a few miles, the ambulance broke down. The driver had realised there was something not quite right so had made radio contact with his base for another one to be sent. It arrived very quickly. The crew were amazing and wasted no time. I felt desperate sitting next to my eight-year-old son lying on a stretcher in the ambulance as he was drifting in and out of consciousness. 'Was he going to survive the trip?' I kept asking myself and pleading with God for help.

As soon as we pulled up at Morriston Hospital, there was a team of doctors and nurses waiting. I have never seen medics move so quickly. They were just amazing. This hospital had been built in 1942 for the American Servicemen. Although at that stage, the building was not as modern as it is today, the care was excellent. They soon realised something serious was happening internally, and I was told they would open him up to see what the problem was. Before they could operate, blood transfusions had to be given as he had been bleeding very heavily internally.

This was very scary. We were told that Roger had lost a huge amount of blood and it was touch and go whether he would make it through the night. It was amazing how God kept us calm at this time. We were offered cigarettes and thanked them but explained that we didn't smoke. They supplied us with cups of tea for which we were very grateful. The Doctor in charge came out several times to see us and on one occasion said, 'I need to inform you that your son has lost a hell of a lot of blood'. He told us that they had arranged for platelets to be flown over from Cardiff. I think he wanted us to realise how serious the situation was as we were quite calm. I guess we were in shock.

It was a situation when we could do nothing but pray. I cannot imagine how other folk cope in a similar situation without being able to pray to a God who cares and supports so wonderfully.

I hated seeing Roger being taken down to the theatre without me. I had always been close to both Paul and Roger's side when they had treatment. The thought of opening him up sounded horrendous. Once Roger had been taken down to Theatre, Arthur and I were shown into some accommodation. This facility was attached to the hospital and had only recently been completed. Parents could stay there if their children were kept in.

That night seemed never-ending as we didn't know what was happening. I was half expecting to be told that he hadn't made it through.

I couldn't bear to think of what life would be like without him. Even though I had three other children, nothing could make up for the loss of one. They were and are equally precious to me. During this long wait, I had been working out in my head what I would put in the obituary column of our local newspaper. At last, I heard footsteps. What were we going to be told? I was expecting to hear that Roger hadn't made it through the operation. Instead, we were told that he had made it through but that there was a long way to go, and he was still on the critical list. They found his spleen had been ruptured in the fall so they had to remove it. We were finally allowed into see him – oh what a shock. He looked awful – grey and lips very pale with lots of tubes going into him. How I wish they had prepared us for what we were about to see.

There followed weeks of massive intravenous Factor 8 injections usually three times a day. The Doctor had put a cannula into the back of his hand which saved having to have a needle going in each time he had an injection. After a few days, he was able to say some words which sounded like gobbledegook. This naturally worried me. Had he suffered brain damage when he hit his head as he landed on a boulder in the stream? I asked the Doctor, and he said it was normal and was a result of the high dose of morphine he had been given. That was a great relief.

Each day was different, some days a very slight improvement and then the next could be a step backwards. Even after quite a few weeks, I was warned several times that he wasn't through the woods yet. The doctors and nurses were excellent; I couldn't praise them enough, and I just thank God for the people he put around my son. Not only were they professional but they were friendly and approachable as well. Although this was not a Haemophilia Centre they seemed to know about this blood disorder and were in regular contact with the specialists in Cardiff Hospital and also St.Thomas.'

After a couple of weeks, Arthur returned home and work, while the other children were still with our friends at their home in Croydon. I had given this family instructions that if Paul had a bleed, they were to take him to St.Thomas' Hospital in London.

I really missed my husband, but I knew he found it difficult to cope with being in the hospital all the time. He felt too that he should go back to work. After Arthur had left, a mother, who was visiting her child, would sometimes put her head round the door and ask if I would like to join her in the canteen for lunch. I would check that it was OK to leave Roger for a short while and then join her. I appreciated this kindness as it was quite lonely a lot of the time. Roger was in a side room, and we were on our own. It was also good to be able to talk to other mothers who had sick children in that hospital. Even if I didn't feel like eating sometimes, I realised it was important that I looked after my own health by having fairly regular meals so that I could care for Roger.

There were several times when things got panicky. One Doctor commented after Roger responded positively to treatment after a crisis; 'There is someone on your side.' I told him that 'Yes, God was on my side.' We got talking, and he told me that he had attended a Billy Graham meeting some years previously.

During this time I had an unexpected visit from an elderly man. He had stayed with us in Maidstone several times. He loved being with our children. Sadly he had lost his wife and four of his children to the Exclusive Brethren. He had heard about Roger's accident and wanted to see for himself how he was. He had travelled all the way from Deal in Kent by coach to see us in Wales. This was such an encouragement to me. It was good to talk with someone that we knew as we were so far from home. He stayed in a hotel overnight and then returned to Deal the following day. He felt satisfied having seen Roger for himself rather than just hearing second-hand news.

It wasn't easy keeping in touch with friends back home as we only had access to the hospital telephone and that wasn't always available. If only we had had mobile phones back then!

It was exhausting sitting by the bedside of my sick son day after day and week after week. Not only was it the very hot summer of 1976 but to make it worse they couldn't turn the central heating off in the hospital! Fortunately, we did have a fan in the room most of the time.

Once Roger was able to take notice I read and reread many Mr Men books to him – he seemed to really enjoy these and so did I! It was great when I was finally told I could lift him out of bed and onto my lap. We had lots of cuddles, just to hold him again was wonderful.

One day I had gone into the parents' room and was on my own in there when I felt as if there was an arm around me. It felt real. I have never forgotten this experience. There was no one else around. I believe it was my Heavenly Father – perhaps He had sent an angel to express His care for me. How I needed the comfort of my Heavenly Father at this time.

After several weeks there were signs of a slow recovery. Our daughter Hilary had been waiting to have her tonsils out for some time and had an appointment that we really felt was important for her to take. We mentioned this to the Doctor who wasn't too sure about allowing Roger home yet. The Doctor asked some nurses to lift him out of bed and holding him, tried to get him to stand. He couldn't stand up and didn't know what to do with his legs. As a result of trying to stand his hip became very swollen and he was in great pain. He had hit that hip on a boulder while falling over the cliff. More treatment needed. As a result of this event, it was doubtful that we would be allowed to take him home the following day. It was a couple of days before Hilary's operation at St.Thomas'.

It was then decided to move Roger into the main Children's Ward. He seemed to settle into his new surroundings, so I decided to pop down to the canteen for a coffee. On returning to the ward, I noticed a smartly dressed gentleman who appeared to be looking for someone.

I asked if I could help and he replied 'I am looking for Mrs Newman.'

I couldn't believe it; he was looking for me! Who could it be as I didn't know anyone in Wales?

I introduced myself, and we got chatting. It happened to be Rev. Arthur Neal who some years before had been the Baptist Minister at Brixham, Devon, where an elderly friend of mine lived, and she had been praying for us. She knew the Minister had moved to South Wales, and she contacted him asking if he could visit us. This visit was a lovely surprise. Although I had never met him, I had read his name in a book called 'From Witchcraft to Christ' by Doreen Irving. He was the Minister who God had used to exorcise many evil spirits from her. We had a lovely time of fellowship together, and he prayed that we would be able to take Roger home the following day. The Lord ministered His peace to me in a special way that day.

After a lot of consultation with St.Thomas' Hospital, it was decided we could take Roger home providing we kept in touch with them. How I was looking forward to getting back and seeing the other children. I had really missed them. Arthur came up so that he could do the driving back home. The journey was tricky as every bump could possibly cause more internal bleeding. We put loads of pillows across the back seat to make it as comfortable as possible for the long journey. When we arrived home, we made a bed up for him in the dining room so that he could be close to us downstairs. We would then carry him upstairs to his bedroom for the nights. He had lost more than a stone in weight. He used to be called 'Rodge the podge'. He certainly didn't look like a podge anymore.

Although all this time in Wales was very traumatic, I felt God's support all the time and am sure He gave me the strength to cope with it all. When we arrived home, we discovered that many people, who we didn't even know, had been praying for Roger. We were so grateful to them and of course to God.

A couple of days after getting home, Arthur took Hilary to St.Thomas' where she had her tonsils out. We were so pleased that we had got back in time to keep this appointment. It wasn't long before she recovered and was able to eat normally.

It was a tremendous responsibility looking after such a weak child without a medical team around. Frequent 'phone calls were made to St.Thomas' until, at last, Roger was strong enough to be taken there. For some time he had daily injections to hopefully prevent any more internal bleeding. Once he was well enough, he had to be taught how to walk again. I used to try and get him to cycle backwards on a bike indoors and also we went to the local swimming baths to hopefully get his legs to work. It was about three months before he could take steps on his own.

Roger had a school friend who lived in the same road as our home, and his mother was a teacher. She kindly agreed to give him some tuition to catch up on some of the lessons he had missed. This extra tuition was a great help, and she made the learning fun.

We had been home a few weeks when we had a visit from the elderly gentleman from Deal who had made that long trek to see us in Wales. He very kindly bought us a portable television. This was amazing, such a generous gift. It gave Roger a real interest when he was unable to do very much. We had never had a television before. In the Exclusive Brethren, this was not allowed and was called 'The devil's eye.'

Chapter 10

Three years after Roger's cliff fall, we had another holiday in South Wales. This time, we stayed well away from the Brecon Beacons! Roger was suffering from jaundice and got so tired he often wanted to be carried. He would say 'Mummy, I've got my hepatitis again.' It caused him considerable fatigue and exhaustion. My husband and I shared the task of carrying him when he was too exhausted to walk. We were constantly looking for seats to sit on and rest for a while. By this time he was getting quite heavy, so we encouraged him to walk a little in between picking him up. The jaundice was caused by Hepatitis B. We are unsure whether he picked this up from the blood transfusions he had in Wales while he was waiting for the operation, or through the Factor 8 products.

When Paul was coming up to eleven years of age, we had a visit from the school doctor who wanted to know where we intended to send both boys for their senior schooling. We had assumed it would be to the comprehensive school opposite to where we lived. We were told that would not be happening and that we should think of a 'special school.' The two possibilities that she suggested to us were Valence School in Westerham, Kent and a special school in Alton, Hampshire. If it were the Valence school, at least I would be able to drive them there on a daily basis. If it were the school in Alton, they would have to attend as boarders. This latter school had specific facilities for haemophiliac boys. Well, I certainly didn't want to move home to Hampshire, and there was no question in my mind of them boarding so far aware from home.

Arthur worked in the Special Education Department of the Kent County Council so he enquired of some of his colleagues if they knew a suitable school. A school was suggested a few miles away from home which we visited. The building was not suitable as there were a lot of stone steps. The headmaster suggested another school in Maidstone where he said the headmistress was sympathetic to those with disabilities. We arranged a visit and, although, a mainstream school, we were very impressed that the headmistress knew about haemophilia and the problems that arise with this disorder. To our great relief, she agreed to accept Paul (and also Roger when he reached the required age). They even arranged for Paul to have all his lessons on the ground floor at the beginning of his first term. He was due to have his ankle fused and would still be in plaster and using crutches. We thanked God for this provision.

The operation to fuse Paul's right ankle was necessary because the constant bleeding had worn away the joint. He was frequently struggling to cope with this either using crutches or a wheelchair. We suspected that he preferred the latter as he could whizz in and out of the rooms of our home and show how he could do 'wheelies'. The operation on his ankle meant he had to stay in St.Thomas' for some time with plenty of Factor 8 cover.

When either boy had to stay in St.Thomas' I preferred to use the train to visit the hospital. I could relax and read a book on the train as opposed to fighting for survival in the traffic. It took a bit of time to get used to the underground, and I found it all rather daunting. On the first occasion, I remember standing in the midst of a crowd and feeling so alone. I didn't know where to go, and I hate getting lost! Finally, I managed to find my way across Westminster Bridge to the Hospital.

Roger had frequent bleeds in his right big toe as he had a habit of stubbing it on stairs or elsewhere. It would be very painful. The bleeding would then spread to the rest of his foot causing him to have difficulty walking. He had a particularly long big toe (like his Dad's!) When he was thirteen the doctors decided that they would operate and shorten the troublesome toe. They would also have to put a screw through to hold it in place. To this day, the screw can still be felt! During his stay in hospital, the nurses placed all the cutlery Roger used into a bucket of bleach on the floor at the bottom of his bed. I felt so angry that they were doing this – inferring that he was UNCLEAN. His bed was in the corner of the ward as if to say 'Keep clear.' To me, this showed ignorance as there was no way hepatitis B or C could be transferred like this. All Roger was concerned about after his operation was the big boot he had to wear to protect the plaster. He was afraid that it would show at his sister's wedding!

In between all these main events, there were the usual bleeds that occurred in joints and muscles. They obviously had to be dealt with quickly to try and prevent too much lasting damage as well as to ease the pain.

We had regular visits to the clinic at St.Thomas'. I found these to be quite depressing as I often encountered other haemophiliacs who were older and who were very disabled. I really dreaded my sons growing up with these disabilities.

It was in the early 1980s that we were asked to transfer to Margate Haemophilia Centre. This move was evidently necessary because of NHS budgeting.

Fortunately, it was a much easier journey from home to Margate, and it was also a much smaller hospital. The staff there were very friendly, and we soon had confidence in them. They not only cared for the medical problems but were interested in the whole person as well as the rest of our family.

In 1984 Paul had many bleeds into the left elbow joint causing it to become very weak and painful. It was suggested that he receive a replacement elbow joint. The procedure was carried out at St.Thomas' and was a particularly painful one because of all the nerves that pass through that joint. This meant, of course, another stay in London and daily visiting. These replacement joints have a finite lifetime, so it was replaced again about twelve years after the first one. To this day he still has to be careful with this elbow.

Chapter 11

It was not long after we had started attending the QEQM in Margate that extra blood tests were carried out. We were not aware of what these were for as they had been having frequent blood tests. From the way they spoke to us, it sounded as if it could be something serious.

We already knew they both had Hepatitis C which they had received through contaminated blood. When they had informed us of that piece of news, It had been difficult to take in. Hepatitis C causes serious damage to the liver and can go on to cause cirrhosis and possibly liver cancer. Now, I wondered whatever next would be revealed.

I finally received a 'phone call from the Doctor saying, 'we have the results of last week's blood test, and I am extremely sorry to have to tell you that both Paul and Roger are HIV positive having received contaminated blood products.'

He went on to say that if I wanted to talk it through to let him know and we could arrange a meeting. Stunned by this news, all I could do was meekly thank him for letting me know. To me, it sounded like a death sentence. It was a massive blow as they had both suffered so much, physically and psychologically, during their young lives. Little was known at this time about the virus, and I did what I could to get as much information as possible. I took a decision not to tell them until they started being interested in girls. When the news came through that they were HIV positive, they were both in their teens.

A few months after this news, I was asked to attend St.Thomas' Hospital as they were preparing to produce a television programme about haemophiliacs who had received contaminated blood products and who were HIV positive as a result. On meeting with the Doctor who had been in charge of their bleeding problems in the past he asked me, 'how have the boys taken the news?'

I replied, 'I decided to wait until they were older and interested in girls before telling them.' He advised me to tell them as soon as possible.

The journey home was really hard as I was thinking how on earth could I tell my sons' such terrible news. I went over and over in my mind how I would be able to break this devastating news to them and when was the best time to tell them. I arrived home that evening while they were still out. They had spent the evening separately with friends. They knew that I had gone to St.Thomas' but they didn't know why.

Paul came home first and asked, 'how did you get on Mum?'

This seemed to be my opportunity to tell him the terrible news. I told him the reason for going to St.Thomas' was to discuss making a programme about haemophiliacs who had received contaminated blood products. While at the hospital, the Doctor who had been looking after him and Roger had said that, sadly, he was HIV positive. There was little response and off he went to bed. Next, Roger came home and asked the same question. I gave him the same account and what I had been told. His reaction was minimal, and then he went off to bed. They would not then have had much idea of the seriousness of this diagnosis. It seemed to take some time for it to sink in and what it would mean to their future.

It was some time after this news that a friend at college asked Roger if he was HIV positive as he knew he had haemophilia. Suddenly the horror of it hit him hard. That evening he was really upset saying that he would never be able to have girlfriends, never get married, never have children, never get a mortgage, never buy a house and never get a job. Reality had really hit home. All he wanted was to be normal and live like everyone else. It was agony for me seeing the torment he was going through.

During the 1980s we were constantly bombarded with news items on the television about AIDS. Also, mention was made of well-known personalities who had died from AIDS. Each time I heard about a death, it felt like a stab in the heart. When was it going to be our turn? I dreaded it happening to one of my sons.

For many years, in my mind, every birthday and Christmas was going to be their last. When given the diagnosis I was told they had a maximum of two or three years to live. As time went on it was hard not knowing whether they had weeks, months or years to live. I started to build up memories that I could hold onto in the future.

One morning, as I was doing the ironing, it suddenly dawned on me that I had actually injected this killer substance into my sons' veins. Horror of horrors; how could I have done such a terrible thing. This thought really got to me. I had to keep reminding myself that I had no way of knowing that the blood product was contaminated. I was supposed to inject them with a substance that would improve their chances of living and not of dying.

With this latest diagnosis, Paul gave up any desire to pursue a career or seek further education. He didn't believe he should make any plans as he didn't have long to live. The diagnosis also meant he was unable to take out life insurance or pay into a pension.

In the early days of AIDS, there was extreme ignorance leading to fear of the virus, and prejudice against those affected. Some American preachers were even calling AIDS a punishment from God. There were reports in The Sun Newspaper that all those with AIDS should be put on an island on their own away from everybody else. Due to the stigma, we had to be very careful who we told. At one time Roger would hide his disability parking disk. He was afraid that someone would ask him why he had it. Even to mention haemophilia might make them assume he had HIV/AIDS.

Wearing my counsellor hat, I decided to attend a training day entitled, 'How to counsel those with HIV/AIDS'.

I attended the session with a Doctor who was also interested in the subject. The course leader wanted to ensure that patients suffering from AIDS did not feel unclean. Feeling inferior was common for these people; very similar, I imagine, to how lepers felt in Biblical times. He then spent a lot of the day explaining how important it was that everything they touched should be wiped down with a rag containing bleach. He also said that we must put on disposable gloves when cleaning. The leader put such an emphasis on this topic that I was beginning to feel quite angry. To me, it was one big contradiction. Carrying on in this way would definitely make them feel unclean. If they didn't see the bleach being applied, they would smell it. I caused a bit of a stir by telling the course leader what I thought! After the day was over the Doctor, who I was with, whisked me away quickly and brought me home.

When we went to stay with a friend for a few days, she asked if we had brought mugs for Paul and Roger to drink out of. She was afraid that AIDS would be passed on to her family. I was also asked if I was afraid of catching AIDS – such ignorance.

One Sunday, about this time, Songs of Praise came from Maidstone. The person speaking, stated in a loud voice; 'you won't find Christians suffering from AIDS.' A local vicar, who knew our situation, was furious and contacted the BBC. He asked for the offending comment to be deleted from the recording. Thankfully they agreed.

Several people, when they heard about what had happened, made comments like 'It's not fair' that is true, it certainly is not fair. Life often isn't fair, particularly when there is suffering as a result of someone else's sin which adds to strong negative feelings. It reminded me of how unfair it was that Jesus died in my place on the cross – He didn't deserve that – I did. However, I am eternally grateful to Him for suffering and dying in my place.

Having been told at the original AIDS diagnosis that they had two or three years to live; every day was precious. Each time they became ill, I feared that this was the beginning of the end. They both suffered from many infections of one sort or another. The anticipation of them possibly dying was almost overwhelming. I thought I would never laugh again or be happy, and that people would avoid speaking to me as they wouldn't know what to say.

They could be quite well one day and the following day, really ill. I remember a friend phoning and in the course of the conversation, he asked me how they were. When I told him Roger was ill again, it appeared from his tone of voice that he doubted me. He said, 'but I only saw him yesterday, and he seemed to be in good form.' This aspect of their illness was very difficult to handle. I felt that this friend thought I was making it up. On another occasion, Paul was ill with a high temperature. A friend called and made this comment to me; 'Oh well, we all have to die sometime.'

I felt so angry at her response; how insensitive can you get. I felt like screaming at her. These were my sons. There have been many times when I have thought of how my Heavenly Father felt knowing what suffering His Son was going to endure. Impossible to comprehend.

One thing that did give me peace was that I knew when their time came to die they would both be going to heaven. That would be their new home. What they would have there would be a lot better than what they had here on earth. Despite this assurance, I still couldn't bear the thought of losing them. In my mind it was the wrong way round – sons or daughters dying before their parents.

They had both trusted Jesus as their Saviour, and their faith helped to keep them going as well as friends and family. I can remember Roger being annoyed that someone had said to him 'If the worse should happen'. His reply was that it would not be the worst. The best was yet to come when he would be with Jesus.

When Paul was twenty years of age, he was extremely weak. His CD4 count had gone down to less than 10. It should be between 500 and 1500. Evidently, due to the HIV, the spleen was eating up the platelets. It meant going to St.Thomas' to have his spleen removed before it was too late. This, of course, is a major operation for anyone, but it is even more dangerous for someone who has haemophilia. Their clotting levels would have to be regularly monitored, and frequent injections of Factor 8 administered to make sure his clotting level was maintained at the correct level. I visited him the day after the operation, and he appeared to have come through as well as could be expected. The day after I received a 'phone call from the hospital to say there were to be no visitors that day; Paul had been rushed down to the theatre again. No explanation was given as to why. It was awful not knowing what was going on with my son, and I hated not being with him. I remember thinking 'Oh well, I might as well go to my usual Homegroup that evening where at least they would all pray for him.'

I haven't a clue what the Bible Study was about as my thoughts were with Paul at St.Thomas', but it was good to be surrounded by caring and prayerful Christian friends. We were finally informed that he had suffered a cardiac arrest. This event, rather naturally, knocked his recovery back.

While they were in the process of removing the spleen, the consultant noticed that Paul had cirrhosis of the liver. This condition had been caused by the Hepatitis C. His notes mention that it was not alcohol induced cirrhosis but active micronodular cirrhosis.

On another occasion, after Paul had suffered for well over a year with a very nasty cough, he came downstairs about ten pm. He had gone to bed not long before. He was white as a sheet and shaking. He had brought up a lot of fresh blood and had burst a blood vessel with his coughing. The first step was to get Factor 8 into him. I then 'phoned Canterbury Hospital who told me to bring him in. The Margate centre had recently been relocated to Canterbury. Normally I didn't drive at night, but my husband had a very early morning taxi job to do taking a client to an airport, and it was too late to cancel. I had no option but to drive him there.

It was usually a 40-minute drive but this time, I got there quicker. It was scary as I was expecting him to slump forward and I was worried that I wouldn't get him there alive. Fortunately, we got there safely, and they settled him in a bed. I could at long last relax. I wasn't sure what I should do. Should I sit by his bed all night or risk driving home in the middle of the night. I decided it was OK to leave, and Paul was happy for me to do so.

I depended on Father God (my Strong Tower) to look after me on the drive home. It was amazing as there was a car in front of me almost all of the way home whose lights I could follow. If he ended up in a ditch, I would have followed! I was very relieved to get home safely after such an arduous night. A friend told me that God must have provided an angel for me to follow. Angel or not I was very relieved to be able to follow that car. It was 2.00am when I eventually arrived home.

During one of Roger's check-ups at St.Thomas,' the Doctor noticed he had a swelling on his neck. He said that he wanted to carry out a biopsy. Roger didn't want to have this done, especially because they said it was to do with his being HIV positive. He felt he could have told them that anyway without the biopsy for which he would have to stay in hospital for a couple of days. He was convinced that it was a total waste of time and would involve unnecessary suffering. When he was discharged, they had omitted to tell him that he was not to drive for a few days. Roger being Roger, got into his car and off he went. Suddenly the road appeared to come up and meet him! The home 'phone went, and a voice said, 'Mum can you please come and pick me up?'

At another check-up, the Doctor felt several lumps in his back. Roger wanted to go to College, and we had discussed this possibility during our visit with the Doctor. He looked at me, said nothing, but the expression on his face gave me his answer. It was saying, 'you won't need to worry about that.'

Both boys suffered from horrible infections on the bottom of their feet. This was a problem that occurred from time to time and caused a lot of pain when walking. Paul also had the nasty skin infection called Molluscum Contagoisum which, although painless, caused unsightly lumps, like small boils, on his face and neck. He was embarrassed to go out as his friends had made one or two comments about them. Some did heal up of their own accord, but those that didn't had to be cut out. He also suffered from thrush as well as numerous warts on his hands.

Chapter 12

During 1996 Paul developed pneumocystis pneumonia. This is a very severe form of pneumonia, from which many of the folk with AIDS have died. From this, he suffered from nausea and night sweats. He used to become very breathless and weak.

Some time after this he asked me to look at his back as it was very painful. I discovered that he had shingles. Again this condition was linked with being HIV positive. After all this he contracted pneumothorax with pneumonia. Pneumothorax is the medical term for a collapsed lung. He had a lot of pain when breathing in. Pleurisy affected him soon after that. It was a really bad year.

Once an HIV positive patient develops pneumocystis pneumonia, the diagnosis is changed to AIDS. So now Paul officially had AIDS. Oh no, I thought; how much longer has he got. It was heartbreaking to see him suffering so much and not being able to do anything about making him better.

He had a poor appetite as he was unable to eat very much. He lost a lot of weight. HIV was sometimes referred to as 'The Slimmer's Disease'.

How I longed for my parents during these years. They would have been the first to come and give me the support I needed. I wrote to them several times over the years to inform them what was happening, but I never got a reply. If they had replied, I am sure they would have said that this was God's judgement on us for leaving the Brethren. On one occasion I was feeling

85

particularly down about not being able to talk to my mother and had been praying. During my prayer session, a voice in my head said, 'I know how you feel; your mother has turned her back on me too.' There was no one else in the house. I just wept, to think she had even treated our loving God in the same way. It made me think of how God must feel when He sees suffering in those He loves so much.

It was when Paul was very ill that he insisted on going to a friend's wedding in London. I tried hard to dissuade him and even asked his Hospital Doctor to persuade him not to go. The Doctor said, 'it's no good, he won't listen to me either.' Paul being Paul, insisted on going to the wedding with his friend Mike. His close friend promised to let me know if Paul got very ill and needed to go home early. He would then 'phone me, and I would immediately travel up to London to bring him home. I sat by the 'phone all that afternoon, and it never rang. You can imagine my relief when Mike brought him home. Mike was such a good friend and support.

It was while Paul was so poorly and spending a lot of time in bed that he was offered a new antiretroviral drug. It was called AZT and was the first of the drugs to be used on HIV/AIDS patients. There were really bad side effects, and some patients refused to take them due to the side effects. Paul agreed to try them although they made him feel quite ill. The side effects were chronic headaches, nausea and debilitating muscle fatigue. Some time after that came a new antiretroviral treatment. It was a triple combination of HIV medicines which have to be taken every day. It was pointed out that this was not a cure but would control the virus. Those who were HIV positive could live a longer and healthier life. Gradually Paul responded to these drugs and grew stronger.

Roger was placed on the triple antiretroviral drugs at a later date.

When Roger was in his twenties, he started giving talks to Doctors, nurses and social workers about what it was like living with HIV. After several monthly talks, he was finding it difficult to take the time off work. He told them that he couldn't continue but that his mother would replace him.Needless to say, he hadn't asked me if I would do it. My reaction was, 'what; I can't speak in public'.

I was terrified of standing up in front of a group of people and giving a talk. After much deliberation, I agreed to give it a go. I would bring in how God and Church friends supported us as a family. After my prepared talk, I always gave an opportunity for questions. The most common one was, 'how do you cope?' Without minimising how hard it was, it gave me the opportunity to share something of God's love and the care shown to my family through many wonderful Christian friends. After several months the NHS decided to discontinue these talks.

One of the hospital nurses, who had attended the talks, had a desire to set up a support group for carers. This nurse's responsibility was dealing with patients who were either HIV positive and/or had Hepatitis C. He was very keen for me to join this carers group. Although I wasn't keen, I felt after praying about it that God wanted me to carry out the role. When I asked Him about it, I was reminded of what Jesus had said about being the salt and light in the world. Perhaps this was an opportunity God had created for me. Although the support group meetings could be quite depressing, it gave me an opportunity to come alongside folk who were going through similar situations to what I had gone through. I was able to share my faith and explain how God had helped through the dark days.

On a few occasions, a couple of young men who were suffering from AIDS joined us. One of them was soon very ill in hospital and wanted me to visit him. I asked his partner if it would be alright for me to visit him and he thought it was a great idea. Oh, this poor young man looked so ill. He was nothing but skin and bone and was obviously very near the end of his life. I shared with him the comfort I had of knowing that when my sons died they would be going to heaven and there is no AIDS there. He listened to what I said about what Jesus had done for our family. How I longed for him to come into God's kingdom. He said he would consider taking the step into the Kingdom when he was nearer the end. My heart sank thinking how much nearer to the end can he get.

He was allowed home for a short time, and I visited him there. Giving him a hug was just like hugging a skeleton. He was also losing his sight. Finally, he was moved into a hospice, and I visited him there. I noticed that he had a Bible open on the table beside his bed. We chatted a little and then I offered to read something from the Bible to him. Unfortunately, someone came into the room to give him treatment, and I had to leave. I then had to go away for a few days. When I got back, his partner told me that just before he died, he had asked to see the chaplain. After that, he had died peacefully.

Perhaps he was like the thief on the cross; a last minute conversion. I trust that was what happened.

There was another couple I befriended in this Carers' Group. They had a son who was homosexual and HIV positive. They were struggling to cope with both of these issues. The wife suffered from quite severe mental health problems and after a few years, they divorced. The husband contacted me very upset about the situation. I continued to try and support him through this difficult time in his life. He became very interested in Christianity and started to attend the Bible Study group that I regularly attended. He also came to my Church on Sunday mornings. Although he had an inquiring mind and therefore many questions, I believe he finally came to know the Lord for himself. Sadly his son died a few years ago.

I had been reading David Watson's book, 'Fear no Evil', which he wrote when suffering from cancer. The only thing I can remember from it was his comment regarding the usual question, 'Why Me'. He said that although it is OK to ask this question, it is more helpful to say, 'Lord what do you want to teach me through this' It made me stop and think about God's purposes in my life. I knew I had still so much to learn. I can honestly say that I have learnt more as a result of going through the illnesses with my sons than I would otherwise have learnt. In fact, I still have got a lot of learning to do.

I do struggle with coming to terms with the fact that God taught me through what happened to my two sons. Why did God allow my sons to suffer in order for me to be changed? It doesn't seem fair. Surely it should have been me affected and not them. I don't understand other than to know that God must have a very good reason and I trust him totally. Sadly there is no way that I can ever change the situation. I will continue to count on God's grace and lean on my strong tower.

One lesson I can still remember is when I attended a talk in the early days of HIV when a Christian Doctor in London talked about homosexuals. This Doctor worked on a ward with very sick AIDS patients. I remember being horrified at the thought of my boys being placed on a ward full of homosexuals. It was a few months after this that I attended a seminar entitled 'Understanding the homosexual'. Although I could never condone their behaviour, God still loves them. If a Holy and Righteous God could love them, then so could I. My view really changed from then on. Since that time I have met quite a few lovely men who are homosexuals. I realised that it is a matter of loving the person, and separating the sin from the person. After all, God loves me, and I am not perfect. Another change in me is that I have learnt to be more compassionate and empathic with others in whatever way they may be hurting and struggling in life.

Both of my sons have had some wonderful friends supporting them through all their bad times, as well as sharing their good times. In particular were a wonderful couple, full of love and laughter, who worked with the youth in our church. They guided them in their Christian walk. They even opened their home to the young people. Although they themselves had a large family, there was always a warm welcome for the youth. In fact, Paul spent quite a lot of time there helping with the children when he wasn't able to work. I will always be grateful for their input.

How I longed and prayed for God to heal my sons. I don't understand why God sometimes heals folk by a miracle and doesn't heal others. I am reconciled to the fact that He is sovereign, and, whichever way He chooses, He must have a reason. My role is to trust Him. What was particularly hard to grasp in this area of healing was when some Christians, who claimed to have a healing ministry, said that healing had taken place after they had prayed over them. Roger firmly believed he had been healed, and on one occasion, told me to get rid of his attendance allowance book as we didn't need it anymore as he was healed. He was shattered when he started having bleeds etc. and realised that he wasn't healed as he still had the medical problems.

This is when our faith can easily be challenged. I have tried to hold on to what God says in Isaiah 43: 'Do not fear, for I have redeemed you;..... When you pass through the waters, I will be with you; and when you pass through the rivers, they will not sweep over you.' I have to admit that sometimes I did feel as if the rivers were sweeping over me.

Equally, I don't understand why God has allowed my sons to live this length of time. Thirty-two years to date, having been told in 1984 that they only had two or three years to live. So far over nine hundred of the haemophiliacs, who received the contaminated blood have died from AIDS out of the twelve hundred infected. Many more of them have died as a result of the Hepatitis C. Several of those were Christians who I had known. Even though I don't understand, I am so incredibly grateful to God that Paul and Roger are still with us. They are such a blessing to us and to those who know them.

Something I believe the Lord challenged me to do as a result of teaching Sunday School children, was to forgive the Government for allowing contaminated blood products to be used on my sons. As a result of their negligence my sons have had to suffer from HIV and Hepatitis C. My own view at the time was that they should be accused of manslaughter. When the Lord showed me I had to forgive these people, whoever they were, I struggled and struggled in real agony for several days. I often said to myself that there was no way I could ever forgive what they had done. I finally gave in and sought to forgive whoever was responsible. The peace that resulted was just amazing. In forgiving, I was not condoning what they had done. I knew that teaching the Sunday School children to obey God I must also obey Him.

A few years ago I visited my G.P. as I have had a chronic cough for many years. A wide diversity of tests and x-rays haven't shown up the cause. Medication would work for a limited amount. On one occasion, my Doctor asked if I had ever had an HIV blood test. I had on several occasions suffered accidental needle pricks while dealing with the boys' intravenous injections. On replying that I hadn't, she recommended that I should have a test. Well, that did it, I was sure I must be HIV positive, and that is why my cough wouldn't clear up. I realised, of course, I was far too old (I was then in my sixties) for them to spend money on the expensive HIV drugs. With this realisation, I started tidying my home, drawers, etc. I was preparing for an early grave.

When the result came through it was with great difficulty that I believed the Doctor that I didn't have HIV; I kept saying 'Are you sure?'

I am glad to say that the result was correct, but I still have the cough!

Against all the odds, Paul married in 1998 and Roger in the previous year. They are married to wonderful girls who are sisters, and they have their own homes and children. Their wives are two very special courageous young ladies. All the things Paul and Roger thought would never happen, have happened. We are so very grateful to God for these miracles.

When Paul got married, we invited his Doctor from the Canterbury Haemophilia Centre, and he accepted the invitation. He commented that it was only a year previously we were planning his funeral. It was during that year that I bumped into a close friend of Paul's in our local Christian Bookshop. He was an itinerant preacher. He told me that he wanted to be at Paul's bedside when he was dying. My husband and I decided we would also like him to take the funeral service. Gladly, we haven't had to call on him.

For many years I kept a list of names and telephone numbers in the back of my Bible, ready to inform folk when the Lord took Paul to his eternal and better home.

In January 2011 both Paul and Roger commenced a year's course of Interferon treatment for the Hepatitis C. This treatment has a similar effect to that of chemotherapy, very unpleasant side effects and no guarantee that it would work.

The liver specialists at Kings College Hospital, London gave them the treatment, and this entailed regular visits. When Paul went to see the Consultant regarding starting this treatment, he mentioned to him that he had cirrhosis of the liver back in 1985, and they had removed his spleen. The Consultant at Kings couldn't believe it. He said, 'If that is true, then you should not be standing in front of me now.'

We believe God had done a miracle healing as they said there was no sign of cirrhosis now. How wonderful is that! Praise the Lord.

During the autumn of this year-long treatment, Roger started getting very breathless. He got very bad, and he had great difficulty getting upstairs or in walking. He became very ill and weak which lasted for some time. The medication he was given didn't seem to be very effective. Evidently, treatment with Interferon can lower the immune system even lower than it was already. After many weeks of illness, he decided to stop the treatment.He immediately started to recover. Recovery took some time, but he decided that he was not going to return to the treatment with Interferon.

Some good news at last! At the beginning of the following year, blood tests were taken and proved that the Hepatitis had gone from both my sons.

Chapter 13

In January 2012 my husband and I had been away with Roger, his wife and children. We all returned home in the afternoon of Friday 6th.

About an hour after we arrived home, Paul had just started driving to Kings College Hospital for a routine liver check-up. Suddenly he had a tremendous pain in his head, and he lost the feeling in his right leg. He managed to 'phone his wife, and she went to pick him up. She spoke to Roger to give him the news. He lived opposite his brother.

Roger realised this was extremely serious. His wife, Linda, rushed Paul to Canterbury Hospital. As soon as he arrived Paul had a brain scan and was then blue lighted all the way to Kings where he was placed in the Intensive Care Unit. He had had a brain aneurysm which is very serious normally but worse with someone with haemophilia. My husband and I went to visit him on Sunday, and he was in an oxygen hood and looked very poorly. He was then in the high dependency unit having been moved out of ITU.

Monday his wife Linda 'phoned me to say his breathing was worse, and he was back in ITU. The following day I went up to see him. He was too weak to speak and was in an oxygen hood to help him breathe. He managed to write a couple of notes to Linda and me. It saddened me to see him looking so poorly.

Wednesday the big shock came. He was now on a life support machine, and we were told he had multiple organ failure. He looked awful; his eyes weren't closed properly, and his tongue was partly out of his mouth. He was connected with tubes and wires to several machines.

I remember sobbing into tissues as I walked on my own to the station that evening, hoping no-one would notice.

The following day the ITU Doctor wanted to speak to Linda, Paul's wife, and me. We followed him into a small room. He explained that he wanted to prepare us for the worst as he didn't think Paul would make it. An hour or two after the meeting, the Liver Specialist also asked to speak to us. He explained to us that he also didn't think Paul would pull through. Although we both realised that it didn't look good for Paul, being warned by two different doctors was quite shattering.

That day all the teams were in attendance, the ITU doctors and nurses, the liver specialist, the HIV/AIDS Consultant and the Haemophilia Doctor. The care that he received was second to none. I have never seen anything so amazing in a hospital. He seemed to have about twenty different tubes going into him.

Several members of our family visited that Thursday. Some had travelled quite a long way to come and pray and give support. The Pastor from Paul's Church also visited and prayed for him. My eldest Grandson's wife was a nurse in Kings College Hospital at the time. When she was on nights, she would try and pop in to see how Paul was doing. She would then 'phone through to Linda. They lived in Peckham at the time so on a few occasions Linda slept there so as to be close to the hospital in case she was urgently needed.

Mark 'phoned through early the next morning to say he had booked his flight from Australia and was leaving that day. We were so glad he was able to come. He arrived safely the following day. He had never seen what goes on in an ITU ward so we warned him what he might see before he visited Paul. There was no change with Paul on that Friday, but at least he wasn't deteriorating. The following day his blood pressure was up a small amount, and he started to open his eyes slightly. This was amazing.

Although his eyes were hazy, the action of opening them gave us a tiny bit of hope. On the Sunday, when he wasn't sleeping, it appeared that he recognised us although he seemed to have difficulty in focusing. In addition to that, it looked as if he understood what people were saying. We knew he was still in a critical condition, but these slight changes gave us hope

On the Monday they were able to take him off the life support machine and stop the dialysis. The Doctors and nurses were encouraged at the progress so far even though he still needed oxygen. They would have witnessed a lot of praying.

The following few days Paul's condition was still very up and down. Our hopes seemed to be raised one moment only to be dashed a while later. One other thing that was causing concern was that there was a blockage related to his liver. As the days progressed, Paul tried to speak a little, but he got very breathless. He was also unable to move his right leg.

The results of some blood tests came through. This confirmed that he had pneumocystis pneumonia.

The following are notes I made in my diary after he had been in hospital for two weeks:-

'Friday: he was much brighter and talked about setting up a business making soup!
The next day his breathing was worse again. His voice was not good either. After a sip of a drink, he was quite sick.

Sunday: slightly better and managed to move his right leg a little.

Monday: he was worse again, liver results were not good, and he was looking a bit yellow. Breathing, much worse and high temperature.

Next day: temperature down a bit and a bit brighter. Started some different antibiotics. He had a small amount of rice and jelly and kept it down.

Wednesday: looking better, colour OK and breathing less laboured. Paul had a small amount of food.

Thursday: he was looking brighter, and breathing was better. Had a small amount of dinner. With the aid of two nurses, he was helped out of bed and was able to sit out for a short time.

The following day, he was moved into a side ward which was still part of ITU. He obviously was getting bored as he fancied doing a crossword.

Sunday: he was sitting out a little longer and his daughter Anna who was six at the time saw her Daddy for the first time in the hospital. She was pleased to see him and of course, Paul was delighted to see his little girl.'

On one of the days, a nurse had left him sitting out too long. As a result, he was very uncomfortable. It was really hard for me as I so wanted to help him back into bed. Doing nurses work would not have been allowed.

We had to spend a lot of time in the Day Room, and there were other families and friends of patients in ITU who were quite distressed. All I could do was pray silently for them. Even though I didn't know them or their situation, I knew that God knew all about them.

There was very little opportunity to speak to any of them.

When Paul was finally moved out of ITU, he was transferred to the Respiratory Ward. He looked better although he was still on oxygen. The staff promptly got him ready with Factor 8 injections to drain off fluid from his abdomen. It had become very swollen and uncomfortable. The procedure was to be carried out under an ultrasound scan the following day. Six litres of fluid were drained off. He was told that there was approximately another six litres to be drained at a later date. Unfortunately, they had forgotten to book him in for a second scan. They explained that it was the liver that was creating the fluid. On the Friday they fitted him in, and they drained off the second lot of fluid. The removal of the fluid helped him to feel more comfortable. He also didn't need to be on Oxygen for as much of the time.

After several weeks a couple of physiotherapists tried to get Paul to stand and to move his legs. This was extremely difficult and watching the performance I really thought he would never walk again. Even if he couldn't walk, it now looked as if we would still have our Paul. For the rest of his time in Kings, he received a considerable amount of physiotherapy.

While in the liver ward, he was told he would have to have an Angiogram. This procedure was required before he could have an operation on his brain to correct the damage caused by the aneurysm. After waiting a week for this to be done, they decided it was too risky to operate on his brain.

After six weeks in Kings, the Doctors discussed the possibility of moving Paul to Canterbury Hospital.

Moving him closer to home would make it much easier for the family to visit. To our surprise and delight, he was told on Monday 20th February that he could go home. This was another answer to prayer and great news. We did wonder how he would cope with going up the stairs; however, he persevered, as he always had done, and slowly got movement back. He was able to walk slowly with the aid of crutches.

A few weeks after Paul had returned home, I decided we should celebrate. An elderly friend, who had known me since I was a baby, had passed away and kindly left me £500. I couldn't think of a better way to use this but to bring together all the family that could make it. I also invited a few of Paul's close friends who had helped during his time in the hospital. I made a reservation for thirty-six in a lovely restaurant where we enjoyed an amazing time of celebration. The event had been kept a secret. Paul's face was a sight to behold when he saw the gathering, especially for him. A friend of mine had made a special 'Welcome Home' cake with a model of a Caterham Super 7 car on top made of icing. We had prayers of thanksgiving to God for what He had done.

Paul carried on his recovery and eventually lived a normal life as if there was nothing wrong with him. Both Paul and Roger have always lived like this. Their Haemophilia Doctor told me that their positive attitude had helped them to cope so well. He also was aware that we were Christians.

After this major traumatic event, life went on reasonably calmly for some time. Paul has been able to enjoy family life as well as work and holidays.

Chapter 14

This time, it was a situation that involved Roger.

Over the years he has had constant bleeds in both ankles; however, the right one caused him the most pain. An Orthopaedic Consultant, who examined him and viewed his X-rays, was amazed that he was still able to walk. The constant bleeds had worn the joint away.

It was decided that the right ankle should be fused. The operation was arranged to be carried out at Canterbury Hospital where they would be able to monitor any bleeding problems. In February 2014, Roger had a rod put through the bottom of his foot and screws through the joint. He was in plaster for six weeks, and the operation seems to have been successful. His other ankle is weak and may in time have to go through a similar procedure. At the moment of writing, he is coping well and working part time.

For a couple of years, Paul has been having regular check-ups for a white spot on the bottom of his tongue. In October 2014 it was confirmed that it had turned cancerous and that an operation would have to be done quickly. Within a few days, he was in the hospital where they had to remove part of his tongue. The surgeon also checked his lymph nodes and had to remove seventy-four. It was done as a precaution and fortunately they found that they were clear of cancer. Speaking caused a problem for some time and eating was particularly difficult and painful.

One evening, about ten days after the operation when he was at home, Paul's tongue started to bleed very heavily. A big and urgent prayer request went round. He looked so pale and shaky. The Consultant at the hospital was contacted, and he decided to increase the Factor 8 and not to re-admit him. Eventually, the bleeding was under control. The problem was that, because it was his tongue, sufficient pressure could not be applied as you would with an external bleed.

Paul was having a really rough time. I felt that poor old Paul had suffered enough from his previous problems without having to go through this new problem. All I could do was plead with God for His mercy for Paul. He is still having monthly check ups and has been told that this will have to continue for at least two years.

Gradually he recovered from this latest setback, and he has continued living an active life with his wife and two children who he adores. He also works part time.

Roger also enjoys a fairly normal life. He works part time and is able to spend time with his wife and three lovely children.

We are now thirty-two years down the road since the diagnosis of HIV and Hepatitis C. The two boys are both on daily medication as well as having antibiotics always available at home, ready for when they pick up any infection. A few years ago they were informed that they had received blood products from someone who had died of vCJD. They have been told that it is unlikely to have any effect on them. I hope that is true.

Paul and Roger, are both amazing in the way in which they have coped with so much. You never hear them complain. They live as if there is nothing wrong with them and are always there to help others. I just praise our God for this. I am incredibly proud of them both.

Living on this roller coaster of emotions I have often been aware that God has been there right next to me holding my right hand. How do I know? Because He says in Isaiah Chapter 14 and verse 13 'For I am the LORD, your God, who takes hold of your right hand and says to you, Do not fear; I will help you.' He certainly has. He has been my Strong Tower on whom I have leant, time and time again.

'The Name of the Lord is a Strong Tower ....' Proverbs 18 verse 10.

I can honestly say that through all the tough times, I have proved what God said to the Apostle Paul 'My grace is sufficient for you...' God provided that grace to me at exactly the time I needed it.

There was nothing else I could do. I had to rely on the One who somehow has sustained me through all these situations. I give Him all the thanks and glory. I wouldn't want to live a second without Him.

APPENDIX

FACTS RELATING TO THE CONTAMINATED BLOOD PRODUCTS

Over the years we have found out that the contaminated blood products originated from American pharmaceutical companies. These companies used to pay donors to provide blood. It appears that to source their donors they used to target groups of vulnerable people who, of course, because of their lifestyles, were highly likely to have infections. This method of sourcing donors had the slang name of *'Harvesting'*. The blood obtained was referred to as *'Liquid Gold'*, due to the high amount of profit that products like Factor 8, could be sold for. It was common practice for these companies to regularly enter prisons and pay inmates for their blood. A lot of these prisoners were already showing signs of major illness, but this was ignored by the people in charge. This blood was then used to generate the products to be used on haemophiliacs in Britain and other countries.

The pharmaceutical company producing the Factor 8, and our Government officials involved at the time, were aware that there was a problem. They rationalised that because it was expensive, it was agreed that it could be used.

Before the disaster took place Dr. David Owen in 1974 decided that if enough money was invested, the UK could become self-sufficient in this area, and blood products would then only come from British sources. More rigid controls could then be enforced, and there would be less likelihood that it would be contaminated.

David Owen announced in the House of Commons that several million pounds had been allocated for this initiative, alas the proposal was not followed up on as the Department of Health was reluctant to invest the money.

This tragedy could have been averted if it was not for greed, deceit, and corruption. The very Government and Department of Health who we relied on to represent our needs and look after our quality of life, allowed my brother and I, as well as many hundreds of others, to be poisoned with contaminated blood. They then washed their hands of any responsibility and tried to bury it.

Since discussions on this tragedy started to unfold, there have been many dubious and sinister incidents. One serious one is where many of the patient's notes were destroyed. When this was raised with the appropriate authorities, they explained that a junior civil servant shredded them in error. A likely story. We have had personal evidence of this as Paul and I obtained a set of our notes and there was a gap where there should have been a record of specific batches of blood products. The record of the batches had clearly been removed.

In the 1980's, haemophiliac patients who had contracted HIV, were asked by the Government to sign an agreement that they would not take legal action against the State for any further infections. This request is likely to have been asked for because they had found out the blood used may have also been contaminated with a Hepatitis C virus. The belief at the time was that those affected with HIV wouldn't live longer than an estimated two or three years. With new drugs etc. life expectancy has increased, but, of course, the authorities weren't aware of this at the time. They hoped that the people affected would die before the other infections affected them. They offered an ex-gratia payment if the people signed the agreement.

There had not been any Public Inquiry into the tragedy until some twenty-five years after the incident took place. Jeffrey Archer finally set up a Public Inquiry seven years ago during which the evidence was clearly spelt out. Many tragic stories were reported. There has never been compensation as this would mean the Government was admitting responsibility. The nearest it has come to accepting responsibility was when David Cameron apologised. After that, a further Inquiry was set up which was called the Penrose Inquiry. This Inquiry was held in Scotland for some reason. It was all a bit of a farce. Some of the victims were so upset by the outcome that they publically burnt copies of the report.

There were debates in Parliament regarding sums of money to help with living expenses. In David Cameron's final speech, he mentioned a sum that was going to be made available to help those affected. Although this sounded a large amount of money, it is actually a pittance when divided between the number of families affected.

Huge numbers of haemophiliacs have died in Britain from AIDS and hundreds more from Hepatitis C. Back in the late 1970's and the early 1980's there were twelve hundred haemophiliacs who had received the contaminated blood and were affected by HIV. Out of that group, more than nine hundred have died. HIV is, of course, the virus that leads on to AIDS. That figure was reported in 2014, so the number who have died will be even higher by now. There were hundreds more of haemophiliacs, given the contaminated blood, who became infected with Hepatitis C. Many more died from this and, in fact, are still dying. These facts and figures are quoted directly from the report in www.taintedblood/info

It has been suggested, by those who know, that this is the biggest tragedy and scandal that has ever occurred in the NHS.

This Appendix has been contributed by Roger Newman. He is from one of the families affected by the tragedy.

August 2016

Printed in Great Britain
by Amazon